PRINCIPLES OF EFT
(EMOTIONAL FREEDOM TECHNIQUES)

other titles in the series

PRINCIPLES OF
THE ALEXANDER TECHNIQUE
Jeremy Chance

PRINCIPLES OF
BACH FLOWER REMEDIES
Stefan Ball

PRINCIPLES OF
CHINESE HERBAL MEDICINE
John Hicks

PRINCIPLES OF
CHINESE MEDICINE
Angela Hicks

PRINCIPLES OF
THE ENNEAGRAM
Karen A. Webb

PRINCIPLES OF
HYPNOTHERAPY
Vera Peiffer

PRINCIPLES OF
KINESIOLOGY
Maggie La Tourelle with Anthea Courtenay

PRINCIPLES OF
NLP
Joseph O'Connor and Ian McDermott

PRINCIPLES OF
REFLEXOLOGY
Nicola Hall

PRINCIPLES OF
REIKI
Kajsa Krishni Boräng

PRINCIPLES OF
TIBETAN MEDICINE
Dr. Tamdin Sither Bradley

PRINCIPLES OF

EFT (EMOTIONAL FREEDOM TECHNIQUES)

What it is, how it works, and what it can do for you

Lawrence Pagett with Paul Millward

FOREWORD BY DR SILVIA HARTMANN

SINGING
DRAGON

LONDON AND PHILADELPHIA

First published in 2014
by Singing Dragon
an imprint of Jessica Kingsley Publishers
73 Collier Street
London N1 9BE, UK
and
400 Market Street, Suite 400
Philadelphia, PA 19106, USA

www.singingdragon.com

Library of Congress Cataloging in Publication Data
A CIP catalog record for this book is available from the Library of Congress

British Library Cataloguing in Publication Data
A CIP catalogue record for this book is available from the British Library

ISBN 978 1 84819 190 7
eISBN 978 0 85701 151 0

Printed and bound in Great Britain

This book is dedicated to Dr Roger Callahan, founder of TFT, Gary Craig, founder of EFT, Dr Silvia Hartmann, founder of EnergyEFT and to God – the founder of all.

DISCLAIMER

1. Absolutely no medical claims are being made to the efficacy of any therapy, advice or processes offered or undertaken within this book. The authors accept no responsibility for the way in which individuals apply the EFT techniques found within these pages.

2. Although the authors have taken considerable care to accurately describe the concepts of meridian-based therapies, no responsibility is taken for any historical or theoretical inaccuracies should they inadvertently arise within the detailed descriptions within this book.

3. The personal views of the authors may or may not reflect the actual views of the individuals cited within *Principles of EFT (Emotional Freedom Techniques)*.

CONTENTS

Foreword by Dr Silvia Hartmann   9

ACKNOWLEDGEMENTS   11

Introduction   13

1   Tracing the Ancient Origins of Asian Energy Concepts   15

2   Historical Exploration of Western Applications of Eastern Energy Modalities   28

3   The Birth of Tapping: Goodheart, Diamond and Callahan   55

4   The Emergence of EFT: The Work of Gary Craig   74

5   The Evolution of EFT: From Craig to Hartmann   95

6   Tapping Into the Power of EFT: DIY EFT for the Beginner   104

7   Real-life Stories of EFT at Work   116

8   What is EnergyEFT? The Work of Dr Silvia Hartmann   128

9   Putting the Energy into EFT: The Practical Benefits of Energy Utilisation   166

10 A Client's Perspective of a
Professional EFT/EnergyEFT
Session   179

BIBLIOGRAPHY   190

LIST OF ORGANISATIONS AND USEFUL CONTACTS   192

Foreword

In this thoughtful and well-researched book, Lawrence Pagett and Paul Millward trace the developmental path that has led us to modern EnergyEFT, before guiding the reader to experience the unique effects of this outstanding change modality for themselves.

EnergyEFT and its theoretical underpinnings present a challenge for those educated, and some might say indoctrinated, into the twentieth-century Western way of thinking. Here, science confines itself to the material and what can be proven in a laboratory; only, there are certain things that are not researched because they are too challenging and too wide ranging.

Science has avoided trying to answer questions such as, 'What is an emotion?' Yet this is a fundamental question, as all things that humans do are driven by emotion, coloured by emotion. Our human lives are all about emotion.

Scientists can become very angry when we start to talk about the energy body; how it produces the phenomenon we call 'emotions' as a direct feedback device to how it is functioning. Yet we must ask, how can we even do clean science without understanding what emotions are, how they work and, especially, how we can control our emotions so that logic, clarity and, most of all, truth may reign in the end.

EFT – Emotional *Freedom* Techniques – is a huge breakthrough for humanity. Before EFT, we were afraid of emotions – of others' and, most of all, of our own. After

EFT, we are no longer afraid. We have a direct tool that can change the way we feel in minutes.

That is entirely unprecedented, and although EFT shares the utilisation of meridians and acupuncture points with the ancient Chinese and Indian traditions, the knowledge of the energy system has never before been applied to human emotions. For humanity, there is no greater topic at this time.

Emotions create wars. They create hatred where there could be love. They create unhappiness, anger, aggression and depression and destroy the lives of men, women and children. They are enormously powerful and, likewise, drive our most important experiences. Emotions are the genesis of all art, all progress and, in the end, all science too.

We cannot begin to estimate just how the world will change as more and more people get to both understand their own emotions and begin to have control over them.

Here I would speak with you directly, dear reader, and ask you to reflect on your own life and how your own emotions have shaped who you are and what you do.

We all have so much potential, strength and power, and it is the barriers that exist within us that hold us back. EFT can break those barriers and set us free, one person at a time.

With every one of us who regains clarity, logic and the will to love, the world changes for the better.

I would lay these pages to follow close to your heart and invite you to an exploration and an adventure like no other – to find out what life can be like when we live in *emotional freedom*.

Dr Silvia Hartmann
Chair, The Association For Meridian and
Energy Therapies (www.theamt.com)
January 2014

ACKNOWLEDGEMENTS

We would like to thank the following: Dr Rupert Sheldrake, biologist and author; Dr Bruce Lipton, biologist and author; Master Zhongxian Wu; Singing Dragon and Jessica Kingsley Publishers; and Ralph James Pagett for his drawings.

Introduction

Principles of EFT (Emotional Freedom Techniques) sets out to give the reader a theoretical and practical step-by-step guide into the fascinating world of meridian-based tapping techniques. Until recently, energy-based interventions like EFT were not widely known; however, even at the time of writing this book, EFT is rapidly capturing the imagination of the general public across the globe.

EFT stands for Emotional Freedom Techniques. It is a tapping procedure, which aims to unblock energy trapped or impeded within the meridian channels of the Energy Body. Energy, when allowed to flow freely, helps to create a positive environment for the healthy, vibrant wellbeing of the planet as a whole. This holistic approach to EFT is grounded within Eastern philosophy and it is imperative to have an understanding of these Eastern sources of energy concepts to appreciate the full power and impact of EFT. It is therefore necessary to trace the ancient origins of Chinese beliefs and traditional healing practices that have existed for thousands of years, because, while EFT may be a relatively new phenomenon, its origins date back to prehistory. Acupuncture, the first meridian-based intervention, is part of this early history where primitive needles made from bian stone were used to bring about physical healing. EFT traces its source from this ancient practice, utilising the same meridian end points for its tapping procedure.

Chapter 2 opens with an exploration of the fundamental difference between Eastern and Western ways of experiencing the world. The Eastern mind encompasses a more harmonious, interconnected relationship towards all life, which stems from a blend of Eastern philosophy and ancient shamanic practices. In contrast, Western thinking has been shaped by scientific reductionist notions that tend to point to a perception of seeing all aspects of life as being separate and independent from each other. For so long, these conflicting views of reality produced stony soil, preventing Eastern energy healing concepts from being planted and nourished in the West. However, this all began to change during the second half of the twentieth century. Chapter 2 posits the intriguing notion that were it not for the turbulent winds of change occurring in the 1960s, then the wasteland that lay between Eastern and Western ideologies may never have been cleared away. It is this pivotal decade that provided the fertile environment for alternative healing practices, like EFT, to blossom freely and flourish.

The theoretical explanation of meridian-based tapping protocols are introduced by first examining the work of Dr Roger Callahan in the form of TFT (Thought Field Therapy) and we go on to describe the work of Gary Craig, the originator of EFT. Finally we enter the curious and magical world of Dr Silvia Hartmann. Along our trip into energy exploration, we invite the reader to join us in learning how to do practical hands-on tapping to enable the reader to become EFT proficient in the three main branches of tapping: Callahan, Craig and Hartmann. It is the authors' hope and intention that by reading this book you will become as captivated and fascinated by EFT as we and the three main players of tapping are.

Additionally, it is our expressed wish that within these pages you may find a wealth of beneficial material to further ignite and energise your EFT adventure…so, when you are ready, take a deep breath, rub your hands briskly together and let the journey begin.

1

Tracing the Ancient Origins of Asian Energy Concepts

The birth of ancient energy healing concepts

The roots of EFT lie in ancient Chinese principles and practices where medicine, spirituality and philosophy are integrated to form a holistic approach to healing. In order to fully appreciate the principles of EFT, one needs to go a very long way back in history. Human concepts of health and wellbeing can be traced back to the Stone Age and beyond. Though life was primitive in those times, there was a tribal necessity for basic human expression in terms of physical bonding, where touching would take prominence for the purposes of keeping warm and protecting one another from hostile influences such as wild animals and other threats.

During that period of time, it was of paramount importance to be physically fit and strong to survive the rigours of daily life. There would be no place for sickness, physical weakness and disability in these harsh environments where one could be literally eaten alive. Simple accidents such as hands being burnt in fires or cuts from sharp stones gave rise to the need to develop basic healing techniques. It was instinctive for these early tribespeople to provide comfort and relief from pain by touching, rubbing and soothing body parts. These natural human attributes of love and compassion gave rise to a desire to heal fellow tribe members of whatever aliments they may be suffering from. This was essential for the preservation and continuance of life.

It was clearly beneficial to early tribal groups to explore, experiment and persist in improving healing practices. This primitive awareness clearly evolved over time and certain individuals began to develop methods of healing on a trial and error basis, retaining methods that worked and discarding those that did not. Over generations these discoveries would have been passed down from family to family and tribe to tribe. Healers would have become highly valued and, in all likelihood, very busy people in this physically demanding and ever-changing world.

The earliest recorded meridian-based healing technique to be used in China was acupuncture, which can be found in the legends that abounded in the ancient literature of the time where it is claimed acupuncture tools were created from stone. In China during the Stone Age period, knives and other implements were used in a therapeutic capacity. These early practitioners came from the East Coast of China. They were pioneering healers who began using needles made out of stone, which they called bian stone.

Conditions in the North of China were very different. Here the climate could be extremely cold and the population was very exposed to high winds. Consequently, people suffered from specific ailments caused by the cold conditions, which were best treated by some form of heat. Over a long period of time, a body of knowledge was acquired through experience, which culminated in a form of heat healing known as moxibustion therapy.

With the advent of the Iron Age, the widespread use of bian stone declined and was replaced by metal acupuncture needles, although the more primitive bian stones are still used today in remote parts of China. The development of these more sophisticated metal needles proved a catalyst for a massive advancement in the practice of a variety of healing techniques including acupuncture, moxibustion, fire needles, warm needling and herbal medicine, all of which were sometimes combined to achieve healing solutions.

The role of shamanism in ancient Chinese civilisation

All ancient civilisations have a history of witchdoctors and shamans (those who are specifically gifted in the art of magical practices such as healing and divination) and China is no exception. These early mystical physicians had an impressive wealth of knowledge, which would have been accumulated from both their personal experience and the shamanic traditions that may have been passed down the ancestral line, both orally and genetically, conferring on them a credibility and pedigree that may be difficult for contemporary Western minds to grasp and appreciate.

The earliest Chinese shamans were known as 'wu' and they date back to the very beginning of Chinese culture. These exceptional people were given responsibility to use their occult powers to serve their tribe's folk and they became a kind of spiritual ambassador, mediating between the hidden mystical realms and the ordinary physical life of the tribe's people. Their practices often took them into other worlds where they travelled, interacted and negotiated with spiritual beings contained within the unseen etheric realms. They were often powerful beings who had learned to experience and handle strong energies. This energetic interaction between worlds was communicated to the ordinary tribespeople through regular ritualised events such as the commonplace staging of religious and healing ceremonies. As a result, encounters with shamans were often powerful, life-changing experiences.

As Chinese culture developed, these Chinese shamans, or wu, began to hold noble positions in the hierarchical structure of tribal society and they became revered by their followers for their wisdom, intelligence and social standing. These deeply spiritual and religious wise men and women took on the combined roles of healers and high priests. The earliest recorded mention of wu can be found during the Shang Dynasty (1600–1046 BC), which marked the beginning of the feudal period of Chinese history. The extent to which the wu were being taken seriously in Chinese society can be seen in the records of the time, which report that ancient Chinese emperors employed shamans to provide them with spiritual information to assist them with important decision making. As a result, shamans played a significant role in the management of the emperor's kingdoms.

During this period, rulers were believed to have direct links to a higher spiritual world, and many of the religious beliefs of the time focused on ancestral spirits. These emperors had authority not only over all aspects of general life in the kingdom, but also over all the spiritual rituals in operation, which were considered to be of paramount importance and in which the shamans would have played a crucial role. It was during the Shang era that shamans were credited as being capable of extraordinary feats such as exorcism, healing and rainmaking.

Ancient shamanistic energy concepts

Shamanism is as relevant today as it was in ancient times. Shamanism's ancient beliefs and practices have been carried down through history to the present day, and contemporary shamans continue to use the same principles and practices. One such present-day practising Chinese shaman is Master Zhongxian Wu, who in his book, *Chinese Shamanic Cosmic Orbit Qigong: Esoteric Talismans, Mantras, and Mudras in Healing and Inner Cultivation* (2010), describes the ancient energy concepts and beliefs that he has inherited from his forbears.

According to Master Wu, the ancient Chinese shamans considered humankind to be a very precious creation deliberately placed on a plane of existence positioned somewhere between the spiritual realms of heaven and the physical reality of life on earth. The key to peace and happiness for the shaman is to find a way of balancing the human body so that a person's heavenly spirit and their earthly physical reality are in unison. The ancient wu discovered that there is an energetic force that fills the whole of creation, which they called Qi energy. This Qi energy (pronounced 'chi') represents the life force and connects together all aspects of nature into oneness: all the way from an individual's internal organs to the furthest reaches of the cosmos.

This life force consists of two forms of energy, which represent the dual aspect of life: heaven and earth. One form of energy is light energy, which represents earth, and the shamans named this *Yin*. The other form of energy is heavy energy, which represents heaven, and they named this *Yang*. These forces of Yin and Yang directly oppose one another, a concept that at first glance seems to suggest a violent world of chaos and uncertainty. However, the concept of Yin and Yang is not one of discord but of harmony: one cannot exist without the other, so without Yin there is no Yang.

When the energetic forces of Yin and Yang are in balance then the universe is in harmony and it achieves a state of unity. When the world is at one in this way, it is reflected in the physical reality of everyday life: communities live together peacefully in a life of abundance and joy. However, when Yin and Yang are not operating in unison then there are imbalances in the cosmic energy system, which is also reflected in the physical world, resulting in warfare, famine, disease, etc.

The ancient shamans discovered that the internal workings of the human body reflected the same energy system as the cosmos at large. This Qi energy consisting of the forces of Yin and Yang forms a matrix connecting all parts of the body, enabling it to function as a whole – both internally and externally – with its environment. According to traditional shamanic thinking, a state of perfect harmony can only be achieved by the individual if he or she blends and merges with the natural forces that surround and govern his life. The individual must become attuned to the natural pulse of life; he or she must literally 'go with the flow', following the eternal stream of life as it surges both within and without them. This concept of how life is energetically organised is an essential concept to grasp if we are to begin to understand the origins of modalities like acupuncture and gain an early insight into EFT.

The shamans viewed the human body as a kind of receptor that could interact with the energies operating in nature and the universe. They came to realise that an individual could obtain internal harmony by getting their body to effectively imitate the balancing forces of Yin and Yang operating in creation at large. With this in mind, they developed a systematic methodology with which to achieve this harmony, which they called Qigong.

The practice of Qigong involves employing a variety of ways of manipulating and working with energy. Much of this revolves around the use of very specific body positions and body movements designed to develop and refine a person's relationship with their internal Qi energy. The practice involves such activities as breathing exercises and meditation and is particularly associated with the use of special hand positions used to create a way of connecting the energy of the universe with the hidden eternal truths that secretly reside within the body, and by so doing, allowing the individual to achieve wisdom and enlightenment. The ancient shaman's practice of Qigong also involved using diagrams and symbols to channel Qi energy to create energy fields with which to heal and re-energise people. The shamans also developed special mantras and vocal sounds to connect with universal Qi energy, to enable the Qi to interact with the body's internal energy system and by so doing, get the person's energy flowing freely to return them to health and wellbeing.

The ancient Chinese shamans, revered as wise sages, held beliefs and practices that form the basis of Chinese philosophy, spirituality and medicine. The shamans' original discovery of the two polarised forces that control the natural world we live in led to the concept of Yin and Yang becoming a cornerstone of Chinese philosophy. Moreover, there is another important strand of the philosophy of Yin and Yang, which also developed from shamanism: the Five Elements Theory.

The Five Elements Theory encompasses an appreciation of the interconnectedness of a whole range of natural phenomena including the seasons, climate, plants and animals. This belief is fundamental to Taoist thinking, which perceives the universe as a totality where everything is considered to be an integral part of the whole. This notion accepts the constantly changing flow of life; a blending, intermingling of forces and forms, which suggests that nothing in life is ever fixed, rigid or static, yet all is interdependent and interconnected.

It can be stated that the Five Elements Theory is naturally observable and can be seen in the changing seasons that blend into one another and how the day subtly shifts into night. The theory takes Wood, Fire, Earth, Metal and Water as the five phases through which Qi energy expresses itself. Qi energy flows endlessly between the five elements and affects the way we respond to our external environment and the forces of nature around us. Each of these elements is associated with specific body parts that can affect our emotions as well as a whole range of other phenomena such as sounds, seasons, colours and taste.

The philosophy of Yin and Yang, coupled with the Five Elements Theory, provides a sophisticated description of the way nature functions, enabling Man to become aware of how delicate the balance of life and nature really is. It emphasises the importance for Man of keeping within the natural harmony that exists between Him and the whole of creation. An understanding of this concept is crucial, if we wish to understand EFT, since it works by manipulating such energy with the aim of balancing the energy forces within the body.

Important historical texts of traditional Chinese medicine

Traditional Chinese medicine has an illustrious history dating back some five thousand years and is closely related to the natural world of shamanism and the ancient concepts of energy they discovered. A very early legendary emperor of China, Fu Hsi (between 4000–2000 BC), was believed to be the country's mythological founder. He is considered to be the author of the Yi Jing (*Book of Changes*), which is the foundation of Chinese philosophy. This significant work contains within it both nature and divination to form a profound wisdom. Its mystical source is intimated by the Chinese legend which tells the shamanic tale of how the book came into being from the markings on the back of a turtle coming out of a river.

However, perhaps the most important book in the history of Chinese medicine is a text that has generally become known as the *Classic of Internal Medicine of the Yellow Emperor.*

The exact origins of this remarkably comprehensive tome are uncertain, but the modern global practice of acupuncture in all its forms can be traced back to this ancient book.

The *Classic of Internal Medicine of the Yellow Emperor* is thought to have been written between 3000 and 2000 years ago and its authorship has been commonly attributed to Huang Ti, the Yellow Emperor; however, it is more likely to have been conceived by a number of individuals. The book describes the philosophy underpinning traditional Chinese medicine and is full of ideas that are as relevant today as they were at the time they were first recorded. The book functions as the academic foundation of traditional Chinese medicine and encompasses not only medicine but also philosophy, mathematics and many other subjects.

Despite the significance of such early texts as the Yellow Emperor book and *The Book of Changes*, it was not until later in history that the golden era of ancient Chinese culture occurred during the 'spring and autumn' period of the Zhou Dynasty (1100–221 BC). This enormously influential period saw the flowering of literature and philosophy when the principles of Taoism and Yin and Yang were formalised in written form. China at this time was a remarkably sophisticated culture and incredibly technologically advanced compared with the Middle East and Europe. The Chinese introduced many innovations and were able to cast large amounts of iron in place of bronze, which enabled them to mass-produce equipment and implements in a way that was unheard of in the West until the Industrial Revolution of the late eighteenth century.

The first acupuncturist medical text was produced circa 360 BC during this fertile era of the 'spring and autumn'. It was called the *Book on Medical Perplexities* and was written by Bian Que, one the great physicians of ancient China. Bian Que was the first man in history to use the pulse for medical purposes and his book prescribed a method of diagnosis that followed four procedures: Observe; Listen; Question; and Pulse Read. Bian Que was remarkably versatile and used a variety of healing techniques including acupuncture, moxibustion, boiled herbal remedies and massage.

Another significant text was written in this period called the *Annals of The Three States*, which documents the legendary herbalist Hua Tuo, circa 160 AD. Hua Tuo developed the use of anaesthetics and used herbal anaesthetics for minor surgeries. He was also the first person in the world to develop a narcotic drug and his extraordinary abilities were 1600 years ahead of the West.

Chinese herbal medicine

Chinese herbal medicine has a long history and is inextricably linked to the natural world of shamanism. The utilisation of herbs for both healing and spiritual purposes has ancient precedents. For example, the vine Yun-Shih (Caesalpinia sepiaria) was the first documented hallucinogenic plant said to possess both medical and magical qualities. The evidence shows that the herb was responsible for allowing the shaman to communicate with the spirit world and even promoted physical levitation.

However, it was the pioneering work of Shen Nong, a legendary Chinese emperor who lived 5000 years ago, which led to the establishment of herbal healing in China. One of the great heroes of ancient Chinese history, Shen Nong was also the inventor of agriculture and was known as the 'Divine Cultivator'. It was Shen Nong who originally identified a large number of plants that could be used for medicinal purposes. He tasted many hundreds of different kinds of plants and drank water from many sources. Legend has it that he was responsible for the first herbal tea tasting when a tealeaf floated into his room and conveniently landed in a pot of freshly boiling water!

It is thought that the knowledge acquired by Shen Nong was handed down orally from generation to generation. The earliest written records of ancient Chinese herbal medicine date from 200 BC where we find a list of 365 healing herbs and remedies, mostly derived from plants. The Chinese identified that herbs have certain individual qualities – salty, sour, bitter, sweet and pungent, each of which have corresponding healing benefits. Moreover, each plant contains life-enhancing Qi energy – the energy that flows through all things in creation.

Chinese herbal medicine developed into two distinct components: academic theory and practical knowledge. The academic knowledge has been created by Chinese scholars, who have formulated a comprehensive body of medical theories. These principles are difficult to comprehend and are open to various interpretations. Nevertheless, despite their academic complexity, they have resulted in the development of an excellent healing methodology: Observe; Listen; and Pulse. The other side is the practical knowledge of herbs that has been uncovered over centuries by generations of the peasant population. Although these two aspects of Chinese herbal medicine appear to be quite distanced from each other, they do in fact complement one another.

Later in our EFT journey we will see the same kind of dichotomy emerging between the professional medical approach to tapping and the layperson's application of meridian-based therapies. We shall see that the seminal work of Roger Callahan epitomises the scientific rigour of diagnostic investigation derived from his background of academic medical professional training, whereas Gary Craig represents a more popular accessible approach, whereby its utilisation is aimed specifically at the ordinary person in the street from a non-medical background. EFT has evolved, and continues to do so, by experimentation, often on a trial and error basis, and this is essentially a very Chinese attitude towards healing. It is both theoretical and practical, both complex and simple, both highly organised and intuitive, and loved by professional practitioners and ordinary folk alike.

The basic understanding of herbal medicine and its applications has altered little over the centuries and can still be seen in evidence in Chinese herbal dispensaries today. Traditional Chinese herbal practices, in keeping with other Chinese healing methods, can be seen to be holistic in approach. The formulation of herbs is complex and a cure may be sought by combining a wide range of herbs. This is a skilful procedure and requires intricate knowledge on behalf of the practitioner. This methodology is non-Western and at odds with Western thinking in that it aims for a broad range of healing when dealing with a specific problem rather than targeting a single symptom.

The practice of acupuncture: directly accessing the meridian energy points

Ancient Chinese medicine is based on the concept that Qi energy flows through channels in the body. For the Chinese, the source of all health problems lies in the disruption of these energy flows in the body, resulting in disease, pain or dysfunction. When this energy is flowing freely, the body can be said to be in good health; when this flow is interrupted, disease and illness may result. These channels of energy are called meridians. It may be helpful to consider meridians as streams of living water: refreshing, revitalising, rejuvenating and irrigating the land. It is important to point out that these energy streams exist within the subtle body and are not visible to conventional Western anatomical analysis.

The purpose of the ancient practice of acupuncture was to restore and maintain this natural flow of energy through the body by interacting with the energy as it moves through this network of channels or meridians. To remove the energy blockages in the body and bring the body back into balance, the acupuncturist would insert needles into the body at certain points along a particular meridian. These needles would either increase the flow of energy or impede the energy flow. This method of inserting needles would continue to be applied until the opposing energies, the Yin and the Yang, were brought back into equilibrium.

This process required immense skill and knowledge on the part of the acupuncturist, whose practices developed into a very complex profession. The Chinese initially identified a total of 71 meridians throughout the body, of which there are 12 main channels, and these relate directly to specific body parts. Additionally, these meridians are connected to one of the Five Elements: Fire, Earth, Water, Wood and Metal. For example: Heart and Small Intestine = Fire Element; Stomach and Spleen = Earth Element; Bladder and Kidney = Water Element; Gallbladder and Liver = Wood Element; Lung and Large Intestine = Metal Element.

Eventually, the Chinese came to believe that over 2000 acupuncture points could be identified on a human body, each of which is connected to 1 of 12 main meridians, or 8 secondary meridians. These channels moved energy between the skin and the internal organs, so it was vital for the acupuncturist to know exactly where to place a needle for it to affect the meridian that had been identified as the location of the problem.

As we shall see in the following chapter, the Western medical establishment had tremendous difficulty believing in this complex system of energy utilisation, as it was completely outside of their framework of training.

2

Historical Exploration of Western Applications of Eastern Energy Modalities

As we have seen, Chinese medicine has a long, distinguished and venerable history whereby the principle phenomenon of energy takes centre stage. It is impossible to understand, either theoretically or practically, the inner workings of the mind and body or the universe as a whole, without an intimate appreciation of this ever-present life force flowing through our world known as Qi energy. It will become clearer as we explore this fascinating topic that this is the fundamental ideological difference between East and West: the East accepts this notion and embraces it with enthusiasm, whereas the West rejects it, even though this energy could be argued to be the prime ingredient of life.

Having looked at the early history of Chinese medicine, we now need to shift our attention to the Western development of medicine and science. It is necessary to briefly examine the basis of the Western tradition in order to understand why the West has so much difficulty in fully grasping the Eastern approach, which is so radically different. This will help to shed light on why it has taken the West so long to take up these Eastern concepts and put them into practice.

The origins of Western medicine can be traced to the ancient Greeks. It was the pioneering thinking of the early Greek philosophers that led to the idea of developing a systematic way of identifying the causes and reasons for the way nature operates. Until Aristotle, science did not actually exist: all intellectual explorations came under the umbrella of philosophy. The split between science and philosophy came from the schism between Aristotle and the Platonic schools of thought with Aristotle's introduction of reasoning and the inception of rationality.

Aristotle was the first significant biologist and is a leading light in the story of Western medicine: he was the father of science and scientific inquiry. However it was Aristotle's students, rather than Aristotle himself, who championed scientific reductionist notions that have led to the study of nature being split into ever-smaller units in an attempt to understand the workings of the universe. One of the disadvantages of this approach is that it tends to assume a rather mechanical outlook where things are seen as separate material pieces within a fixed solid structure held in place by time and space.

Applying this to the study of the anatomy has led Western thought to perceive the body like it is a frozen sculpture separate from its environment, which can be analysed and classified by cutting it up into smaller and smaller sections, segments and pieces. This raises an essential distinction between Western and Eastern minds. To Eastern sensibilities this atomic fragmentation makes little sense and tends to degrade the unified splendour of a creation flowing and teeming with life. It is directly opposed to Chinese energy concepts.

The inherent danger of the Western scientific approach is that it fails to appreciate the essence or essential nature of an entity and its energetic relationship to its environment. Although the aim is to gain a more precise and comprehensive scientific evaluation of the entity and how it functions by making these ever finer and detailed distinctions in an attempt to get to the 'bottom of the mystery', this endeavour invariably raises more questions than it answers and takes the inquiry and inquirer further from the essential truth.

For example, Western science has discovered that the average adult human body contains approximately 6.7×10^{27} atoms and consists of approximately 60 chemical elements. We can list all these elements and calculate their percentage of mass and also their atomic percentage, yet what does this really teach us? It appears to point to an absurd conclusion that a human being is merely a collection of chemicals and atoms and in the final analysis can be summed up as little more than a handful of dust.

In his cult book *Zen and the Art of Motorcycle Maintenance* (1974), writer and philosopher Robert Pirsig describes in detail how the ancient Greek philosophers originally developed the methodology of scientific inquiry that is still the basis of the scientific procedure in use today. Scientific approach requires the establishment of a hypothesis for which evidence is then accumulated to support the hypothesis. Once a certain amount of evidence has been collected, the hypothesis is accepted as being true (a process that is in itself incredibly subjective). The problem with this approach, as pointed out by Pirsig, is that for any particular observation in the natural world, there are any number of hypotheses that could be put forward to explain the behaviour of that particular phenomenon, and evidence could be found to support any one of these hypotheses. Pirsig argues that rather than leading us to absolute truth, science simply provides a myriad of alternative 'truths'.

Western medicine has developed a concept of anatomy, which has been gained primarily from the study and analysis of deceased bodies. However, this method of enquiry is fundamentally flawed. We are seeking to heal living bodies not deceased ones, and a living body is a very different entity to a dead one! It is clear that within a corpse there is an absence of life, and the vital life energy that the Chinese doctors recognise as Qi seems to be entirely excluded by medical practitioners of the West and from traditional forms of Western medicine. This could be considered an astonishing oversight, for how can we heal a living body and mind without taking into account the energy forces at work within them?

Ancient Chinese medicine has an impressive heritage and a comprehensive appreciation of physiology and anatomy. Interestingly, it also has a history of dissecting corpses in the pursuit of anatomic discovery. Nevertheless, unlike its Western counterparts, its energy concepts offer a way to appreciate the bigger picture and show how the quintessential essence of the body is held together in harmony, flow and balance with the external environment. This understanding of the world allows room in its belief structure for a holistic and integrated reverence for life.

We can now see clearly that the Chinese and Western understandings of how the body works are fundamentally different and incomparable. The reasons for this are partly cultural, philosophical and ideologically based. Additionally, these differences express themselves further in their differing styles of research and validation of data, and the very nature of what science is can be called into question. It certainly helps explain why practices such as acupuncture, which have been practised in China for thousands of years, were until relatively recently, completely unknown in the West.

One of the fundamental problems Western science has with understanding Eastern energy concepts is that it is still operating in the context of Newtonian physics, which implies an entirely deterministic universe rather than a dynamic one governed by the unpredictable behaviour of energy. In the seventeenth century Isaac Newton ingeniously developed a complete model of the universe where solid objects moved through space according to mathematical laws of motion. In Newton's physics the universe is a mechanical system where solid objects move in a uniform manner through three-dimensional space and linear time. Everything that occurs in this universe comes from the interaction of separate mechanical pieces, which can be predicted with absolute precision.

Newton was, without doubt, a man of extraordinary genius who continues to be held in the highest esteem by the scientific community. However, Newtonian physics has had the unfortunate effect of reducing reality and the universe to a mechanical clockwork machine: a predictable world as solid as concrete. However, amazing developments in physics during the early decades of the twentieth century completely undermined the Newtonian world view. Despite the fact that modern physics has proved Newton's theories to be false, conventional Western culture has remained stuck in the materialistic, mechanical world of Newton. The irresistible illusion of Newton's clockwork universe has held the educated masses under its spell for three centuries now. It has become so deeply embedded within the fabric of our culture and belief systems, that although Western science has, since 1900, developed a completely new physics that entirely negates Newton's laws, Newtonian attitudes continue to shape our thinking, perpetuating the myth that a human being is nothing more than a solid, mechanical object separate to other similarly isolated human beings.

This Newtonian world view is so potent and so deeply ingrained in the Western mind that it continues to dominate the mindset of not only the public at large, but also the one group of people that has less excuse than any other to continue with such out-dated thinking − the scientific community itself, which still largely sees the world through Newtonian eyes. A major stumbling block in moving science away from such obsolete thinking is the fact that Newton's laws and equations provide a close enough approximation to the way nature behaves in reality for it to be continued to be used in many everyday, practical situations, particularly in the world of engineering. For the sake of its ease of application, the relatively simple mathematics of Newton's physics ensures its continued widespread use despite the fact that the principles upon which it is based are wrong.

However, this static, inflexible world view does not reflect the true nature of life. As we will see in the next part of this chapter, it certainly does not reflect the rich cultural vibrancy that exploded in the 1960s or the rich eclectic variety of art, music, philosophy and spirituality that has emerged and continues to blossom from the New Age movement. Perhaps more importantly for our purposes, it certainly has no place in the world of EFT.

It can be shown that the credibility of much traditional Western science rests upon quite unsubstantiated assumptions that have become sacrosanct laws within the Western scientific community and are readily accepted by society at large. The eminent English Cambridge University biologist Dr Rupert Sheldrake argues that Western science has become dogmatic and that this has had the negative effect of preventing science from evolving. According to

Sheldrake (2012), there are ten main dogmas of Western science, which can be outlined as follows:

1. Nature is mechanical and everything contained within it is like a machine. Humans are therefore mere machines.

2. The universe is unconscious and made up of unconscious matter. There is no consciousness in Man, plants, animals, the stars and the cosmos.

3. The laws of nature and constants are fixed. They cannot be altered.

4. The total matter and energy of the universe never changes in quantity. It all came from nowhere in an instant when the Big Bang exploded it into being.

5. Nature has no purpose – the process of evolution has no purpose.

6. All biological inheritance is material.

7. Memories are stored inside your brain.

8. Mind is inside your head. All activity is only within the brain.

9. All psychic phenomena are impossible. There is no such thing as the paranormal.

10. Mechanistic medicine is the only medicine that is efficacious. Complementary and alternative medicine is ineffective.

(pp.7–8)

According to Sheldrake, these ideas are highly questionable and none of them stand up particularly well to scientific scrutiny. Sheldrake's views suggests there is a crisis at the very heart of science today, which hinges on the contradiction that exists between science as a wholly objective investigation to discover truth based on reason and evidence, and science as a belief system that presents a certain rigid world view.

This fixed, rigid structure of traditional science prevents us from exploring alternative medicines; sickness, old age and death are inevitable in this materialistic world, and they can only be at best temporarily relieved by allopathic medicine. This is not the spirit of the New Age and it bears no resemblance to the spiritual optimism of eternal life offered by the wide spectrum of faiths that exist in both the West and the East. As Sheldrake says:

> The science delusion is the belief that science already understands the nature of reality in principle, leaving only the details to be filled in…It's the kind of belief system of people who say I don't believe in God, I believe in science. It's a belief system which has now been spread to the entire world. (Sheldrake 2013)

Creating the environment for Eastern practices in the West: the 1960s and the New Age movement

It is tempting to assume that with all the technological advances that took place in the 1960s Western science became unassailable. However, the success of acupuncture and Eastern medicine over many generations in the East does raise doubts over the assumed superiority that the West supposedly had. Ancient Chinese medicine has an impressive heritage and a comprehensive appreciation of both physiology and anatomy, which could not be easily dismissed; unfortunately its energy concepts were alien to Western thinking and proved a stumbling block to understanding the Eastern attitude to health. With such a polarity of approach between the two sides there seemed little hope of any kind of reconciliation, and it is arguable that were it not for the counterculture that emerged in 1960s America, Eastern philosophy and medicine would still be largely unknown in Western culture.

The refreshing new environment that emerged in the 1960s was fertile ground for New Age philosophy to take root and flourish in the decades that followed. The growing popularity of New Age thinking in recent years has been one of the most important factors in bringing an understanding of Eastern energy concepts to people in the West. The rise of the New Age movement has resulted in many Eastern healing techniques being adapted and applied in practice by progressive Western doctors.

However, it would be wrong to assume that the New Age philosophy was born purely out of the 1960s counterculture. There have been radical thinkers of a New Age persuasion challenging the Western materialistic world view for some three centuries. The expression 'New Age' was first used as far back as 1809 by William Blake in his preface to *Milton a Poem:* 'Rouze up oh young Men of the New Age!' (Essick and Viscomi 1998, p.319). This preface also included the poem 'And did those feet in ancient time', the words of which later became the lyrics to the immortal hymn 'Jerusalem'.

Blake was well known for his dreams, visions and communication with the heavenly realms of angels and biblical Old Testament prophets. The biblical stories containing miracles, angels and demons were real to Blake. The divine painter and poet's world seemed to inhabit such realities without contradiction.

Blake was a Christian visionary who believed that a new era of spiritual and artistic enlightenment was beckoning. He was greatly influenced by the writings of Swedish Christian mystic and scientist Emanuel Swedenborg who believed in an imminent Christian spiritual awakening. Swedenborg also believed that celestial beings were all around us and were actually visible to those with an attuned sensitivity to such spiritual realities.

However, it was during the nineteenth century that many of the basic features of New Age thinking first emerged through the development of such movements as spiritualism and theosophy. This led to new approaches to scientific practices in medicine giving rise to alternative disciplines such as chiropractic and naturopathy. These ideas also influenced the new Christian socialist movement and in 1894 a Christian journal promoting socialism, *The New Age*, was published.

The great Swiss psychologist Carl Jung was, interestingly, a believer in the Age of Aquarius long before it was taken up by the hippies of the 1960s. Jung wrote a letter in which he mentioned: '1940 is the year when we approach the meridian of the first star in Aquarius. It is the premonitory earthquake of the New Age' (Dr Z 2013).

However, it was in the 1960s that the possible significance of the Age of Aquarius first came to the attention of the general public. It was during this decade of immense upheaval that a significant proportion of the youth of America began to question everything that Western society had come to represent. Hippies rejected many of its country's most cherished notions and rebelled against the very things that had brought America so much success: capitalism, materialism and conventional practices of all kinds were suddenly being vilified by a disillusioned youth, appalled by their country's involvement in Vietnam and determined to forge a new of way of life based on the more enlightened concepts of peace, brotherhood and spirituality.

This wholesale questioning of the older generation's mishandling of its powers also included a growing mistrust of the seemingly unassailable status that science seemed to hold over Western thinking. For the first time, professional experts were no longer treated like gods whose every word was revered as indefatigable truth. Confidence in conventional science started to wane as its devastating effects on the environment began to be noticed by many in the counterculture and people began to protest passionately against the use of chemicals and pesticides. A similar process of disillusionment took place within the field of medicine with many people's faith in doctors beginning to fail as the devastating side effects of prescribed drugs became more obvious to the public, particularly the disastrous thalidomide scandal, which haunts the profession to this day.

Having rejected their own figures of authority, the hippies turned to the gurus of the East for guidance and leadership. The most famous of these was the Maharishi, a charismatic Indian Yogi who achieved celebrity status in the West in the 1960s. The widespread discovery of Transcendental Meditation in America during the decade was due in large part to the Maharishi, who made the practice of meditation a simple and accessible discipline for those seeking spiritual enlightenment.

However, Transcendental Meditation may well have remained relatively unknown in the West if the Beatles had not decided to appoint the Maharishi as their spiritual guru. The time they spent in India with the Maharishi received massive worldwide exposure. It created enormous interest and excitement, and it proved to be a catalyst that inspired thousands of young American, British and European people to explore Eastern spirituality and culture.

As the 1960s progressed, the Beatles naturally found themselves the unofficial spokesmen for the counterculture: their influence in turning the West on to all things Eastern is incalculable. Just by simply visiting India, the Beatles had done more to break down the cultural barriers between East and West than anything previously seen in history. Almost instantaneously, the youth of America and the UK began embracing many forms of Eastern mysticism including Taoism and Zen Buddhism, many of them dropping out of conventional society to embark upon spiritual quests to the East, particularly India. Suddenly it was cool to take up yoga, listen to the sitar and meditate your way into cosmic bliss. In just a few short years, techniques that had been practised in the East for thousands of years were being assimilated by progressive Westerners, influencing a whole range of disciplines in art and science including medicine, psychology music and literature.

One well-known writer of the era was anthropologist Carlos Castaneda, who through his chronicled experiences with legendary Mexican sorcerer Don Juan, did much to popularise shamanic traditions. He wrote a number of books outlining his time spent under the authority of Don Juan where the bumbling, self-effacing novice trained to be a sorcerer's apprentice. Through these ancient traditions and teachings we are given an insight into Mexican shamanic ways: exotic plants and substances like mescaline deriving from the peyote cactus were used to create altered states of consciousness (ASC) where Don Juan introduced his subject to strange beings from other worlds. A very amusing example is when Castaneda, under the influence of peyote, encountered Mescalitos, the god of mescaline, in the form of a dog and at another time he appeared in the form of a giant green cactus.

On the subject of mind-altering substances, Castaneda insists that these plants do not create hallucinations in those who take them; conversely they remove the hallucinations of ordinary people's perceptions and enable the participant to truly 'see'. To the shaman it is the everyday life of the average person that is illusion.

Castaneda was quickly elevated to iconic status by his followers in the 1960s, achieving legendary status and influencing a whole generation. To this day he holds the title of 'The Godfather of the American New Age'. Clearly the mystical use of drugs fitted perfectly with the trendy hippies' own psychedelic experimentation of the time. Moreover, the accounts of Juan Matus, the Yaqui Indian, continue to impact on the spiritually minded today.

Whether these fantastical tales that Castaneda recounted were grounded in fact and whether or not Don Juan really existed are fiercely contested. However, such details are not particularly relevant for the purposes of tracing the ancient origins of EFT, for by its very definition, shamanism deliberately challenges people's cherished notions and beliefs. The shaman seeks to question the static malaise of conventional thinking and behaviour. It is the role of the shaman to deconstruct limiting world views and open up its followers to alternative realities and new ways of perceiving life. Indeed, these otherworldly realities and so-called objective fact, fantasy and fiction are blended and fused together. They are all inseparable to the shaman and form a potent brew for the human psyche to feed on: a wonderful concoction for those who wish to evolve and extend their boundaries.

Castaneda's comprehensive and ever-popular body of work is considered an outstanding work of literary genius. Although it comes from a Western anthropologist's perspective, many of the facts seem fabricated or are possibly blatant lies. However, to this day, the publishers Simon and Schuster continue to catalogue the books under 'non fiction' and these documents describe tried and tested magical methodologies that are extremely useful to anyone wishing to explore alternative realities and shamanic practices.

Another significant writer who introduced Eastern thinking to the West is Jack Kerouac, whose critically acclaimed seminal book *On the Road* (1957), is said to be the voice of the generation. It reveals a literary world far removed from Western everyday life and sums up the Eastern philosophy that had captivated the hearts and minds of the 1960s children:

> I had reached the point of ecstasy that I always wanted to reach, which was the complete step across chronological time into timeless shadows…and myself hurrying to a plank where all the angels dove off and flew into the holy void of uncreated emptiness, the potent and inconceivable radiancies shining in bright Mind Essence, innumerable lotuslands falling open in the magic mothswarm of heaven. I could hear an indescribable seething roar which wasn't in my ear but everywhere and had nothing to do with sounds. (Kerouac 1957, pp.156–157)

Additionally, Jewish intellectual, poet and fellow Beat writer Allen Ginsberg travelled to India in 1963, where he became enlightened by studying alongside religious monks. The Beat generation had faith in Eastern spirituality, believing that it would help to raise Western consciousness higher and that its concepts of unity and spiritual oneness were an essential part of the Beat generation.

To sum up, the 1960s was a time of youthful rebellion against the conventions of Western society, where the young generation enthusiastically began embracing Eastern concepts. In fact, they were hungry for these alternative ideas and this new refreshing environment was fertile ground for the New Age philosophy to take root and flourish.

The spiritual New Age movement evolved from the counterculture of the 1960s and is one of the most positive things that came out of this influential period. It gradually emerged as an underground movement during the 1970s, but it did not at this time have sufficient impact on mainstream society to challenge the prevailing Western ideologies that were still rooted in Aristotle's reductive influence. Even as late as the early 1980s, New Age thinking was largely absent from general consensual reality. It certainly was not the prevailing spirit of the time. The Reagan–Thatcher era was one of intense materialism, with little room for spiritual values and compassion. In the UK at least, this energetically depressing time was further reflected in the unemployment dole queues, class warfare between unions and employers, and the appearance of AIDS.

It is not altogether clear why the vibrancy of the 1960s had all but vanished. Its critics could have concluded at that time that it was merely a frothy passing phase of youthful idealism, the seeds of which had fallen predominantly on deaf ears and stony ground, now apparently discarded by the very generation who had sown them. Yet, in hindsight it would perhaps be more accurate to view this as a seasonal fluctuation where the fecundity of the spring of the 1960s and halcyon summer days of the 1970s had necessarily cycled into a period of winter respite.

Sometime towards the end of the 1980s there was a definite energetic shift and in the 1990s the New Age movement began to make its presence felt. The UK prime minister Margaret Thatcher resigned after attempting to implement an unfair system in the form of the Poll Tax, and from a New Age perspective it was as if the cosmos sighed with relief. This breath of fresh air swept through the UK and was clearly discernible to the energy conscious among us. The New Age spring had sprung: the dawning of Aquarius had begun.

There was a lighter, refreshing quality to life. Suddenly it was curiously fashionable and trendy once more to believe in all forms of the supernatural. Ghosts, fairies and witches became credible. Moreover, God became popular, with the explosion of the Christian Charismatic movement with its emphasis on The Holy Spirit. New Age spiritual self-help books and subjects about near death experiences (NDEs) became mainstream bestsellers. A new generation was born, in which the youth seemed kinder and more affectionate towards one another. The rise of techno dance music and instrumental trance music reflected the old psychedelic hippie values of love not war and the new generation embraced the virtues of green ecology and the global village.

The New Age movement did have its critics though. Mainstream Christianity largely viewed it with suspicion, condemning its practices and philosophies out of hand, believing it to be anti-God. Secular views considered its occult origins as dubious and its activities as a collection of quasi-religious practices bordering on the delusional. When herbal tea was first sold in health shops it was frowned upon and seen as harkening back to Pagan ritualisation.

Despite these objections, the New Age movement continued to flourish and gather momentum. Although still considered with scepticism among more conservative minds, the dam finally burst its banks inviting an ever-present flow of refreshing spiritual streams gently touching society and irrigating the parched land, ridding it of much of its outmoded spiritual aridity. This life-enhancing energy began to water the seeds sown by the 1960s love and peace generation and flowers began blooming, with oases appearing from the mists like mirages among the sandy deserts that had previously been constructed and inhabited by rational Western minds.

Eastern concepts were slowly becoming culturally integrated into mainstream awareness. Prevailing attitudes were changing and Chinese energy concepts were being explored and expressed in a variety of ways. The yoga classes that sprung up in every town in the 1960s and 1970s and the ever-more popular kung fu and karate martial arts centres are indications of this energetic shift. New Age spirituality began to become fashionable among celebrities and was embraced by the general public. Consciousness has observably been steadily rising since then.

These refreshing new attitudes that have created a more relaxed and tolerant atmosphere began providing a much happier and far more optimistic environment for people to explore new ideas and practices. Creativity could now thrive in this new spiritual landscape and therefore it is no surprise that novel therapies and healing modalities began to develop out of this fertile ground. The result was that Eastern religions and Asian medical practices were far more accessible to the layperson, with the growing significance of the internet contributing to the emerging Western appreciation of Eastern philosophy, spirituality and healing practices. For the first time Eastern medical practices were becoming accessible to the layperson. Ancient traditional healing modalities like acupuncture, moxibustion and Chinese herbalism were becoming known and practised in the West for the first time.

Einstein, quantum physics and the New Age

Although quantum physics was first developed in the early decades of the twentieth century, its discoveries were so bizarre and baffling to the rationalist mind that the deeper implications it had for the true nature of reality were not initially recognised. It was not until much later in the century that the discovery of the quantum world had profound repercussions in the wider world when the New Age began to examine the philosophical implications of this new physics. The New Age community realised that the advent of quantum physics returned the world to a much more uncertain and mysterious condition: a fluid world that was far from being predictable.

Quantum physics has revealed that the supposedly solid world we inhabit is made up of tiny sub-particles held together in spatial relationships by fields of energy. Western science had finally uncovered something that the East has known since ancient times: the whole universe is made of energy. Matter could no longer be viewed as fixed and solid; indeed Einstein's theories had already indicated that matter is actually pure energy. His famous equation $E = MC^2$ revealed that even the smallest of objects hold within them massive amounts of energy.

Experiments with particles at the quantum level have proved that we cannot predict their behaviour with any certainty; we can only predict a range of possible outcomes called probability waves. It is the very act of observing these particles that collapses the probability wave into a fixed position. *In other words, the act of observing the world changes the world: there is no measurable objective reality that can be dissected and analysed to ascertain truth.* A single human being, be he scientist or poet, cannot detach himself from his environment: both observer and the observed are constantly acting upon each other.

It is a great irony that Western science (which had put so much faith in a methodology that required everything in nature to be split up and separately identified) had now proved to itself that separation was a fallacy. Quantum physics proved that every single component in creation is connected to every other. The Western Rationalists had unintentionally provided empirically based evidence to support ancient Eastern spiritual beliefs about the unity of creation, and within the context of Chinese medical practices, quantum physics proved that these Eastern practitioners were absolutely correct in the importance they place on taking a holistic approach towards healing the body.

Western science was now being forced by its own discoveries to acknowledge the existence of invisible forces that underpinned reality. It was unwittingly dismantling Newton's deterministic universe in favour of something that was unexpectedly much closer to the Eastern spiritual tradition. Indeed, it was this unlikely connection that the New Age movement recognised, seizing upon this radical new physics to complement and reinforce its own discoveries of ancient Eastern beliefs.

In the old Newtonian physics, energy played no part in the way molecules interact with each other. Therefore the body's cells could only be acted upon by other pieces of matter such as drugs. Quantum physics has shown that molecules are not solid pieces of matter but are energy fields, which can be acted upon, not only by other molecules, but also by invisible energy waves.

The biologist Dr Bruce Lipton, author of *The Biology of Belief* (2005), realised the whole approach that conventional medicine had towards healing was wrong when he worked as a young researcher cloning cells. Lipton argues that biology is still operating within the Newtonian world where bits of matter are assembled together in a mechanical way. It still does not take into account the concept of energy – the very force that drives everything in the universe. In his view this makes biology 'unscientific' because it ignores the discoveries of quantum physics, which have shown that everything in nature is being controlled by these invisible moving forces, which have been identified as energy fields. As a result, conventional medicine remains fixated on the use of drugs to cure everything, instead of attempting to ascertain the way in which these energy fields may be affecting the health of an individual.

Western science is further challenged by New Age scientist reformers

The energy-rich vibrancy of the New Age, which originally emerged during the post 1960s era, has played a significant role in spreading Eastern philosophy and spiritual practices to the West. From the New Age movement a thriving eclectic community has sprung, buzzing with life and a new generation of more avant-garde scientists have grown from this fresh fertile soil. People such as Sheldrake and Lipton are part of a growing army of Western scientists who have managed to extricate themselves from Western materialistic dogmas by broadening their minds and outlook by studying and absorbing the progressive science of people such as Albert Einstein and the exotic theories of quantum physics. This new breed of scientist is questioning the very nature of science itself: indeed they have started a process of redefining what science actually is.

To their minds, the overemphasis placed on the exaggerated self-importance of Western scientific thinking, including all its presuppositions and reductionist conclusions, have invariably led to a largely unsubstantiated scientific world view that claims fallaciously that Western orthodox science is beyond doubt and must be accepted as fact not theory. As this book deals with the principles of EFT, a successful and popular alternative and complementary therapy, it is important to underline and emphasise that these entrenched notions held by Western science over many years are erroneous.

In the context of this cultural revolution, Robert Pirsig's *Zen and the Art of Motorcycle Maintenance* (1974) has been hugely influential in highlighting the inherent flaws of the Western scientific methodology. Pirsig is a classic example of an academic coming out of the environment of the 1960s, who greatly helped bring Eastern philosophical and spiritual concepts to the West. It is difficult to underplay the significance of this book in the context of it being at the right place at the right time to disseminate its Eastern wisdom to those who 'have eyes to see and ears to hear'.

The dogmatic assumptions upon which traditional Western science is based are now rightly being challenged by serious academics and scientists and are being found to be inaccurate and unscientific. We are hopefully reaching a point in history where these dogmas will be recognised by the wider scientific community as being totally unsustainable, and the outmoded concepts that science is based on will be seen by the wider society for what they truly are – largely unsubstantiated claims that fail to take into consideration the bigger picture.

The weight of evidence against them is mounting. Let us take Rupert Sheldrake's dogma number nine, which was outlined earlier in this chapter as an example: 'There is no such thing as paranormal activity' (Sheldrake 2012, p.8). Parapsychology, the scientific study of the paranormal, is largely dismissed by the present scientific community, despite the fact that there is an abundance of scientific evidence for it. Parapsychology writer and investigator Robert Mcluhan, a rigorous researcher and expert on such matters, concludes in his excellent book, *The Randi's Prize: What Sceptics Say About the Paranormal, Why they are Wrong and Why it Matters* (2010), that there is voluminous scientific evidence for the supernatural and that those who refute this are incapable of offering satisfactory evidence to the contrary. Both Sheldrake's and Mcluhan's work brings convincing arguments to the table that show that sceptics are not impartial observers in such matters and have a misplaced faith in the science of reason.

The supernatural cannot be so easily explained away as the materialists would like. It is fundamental to all the major religions, which always have believed and always will believe in the supernatural. Mainstream Christianity, for example, places the historical Resurrection of Jesus Christ at the heart of its faith. It did so 2000 years ago, it does so to this day and will surely continue to do so many years from now. Moreover, the miracles that formed the basis of Christ's teachings are considered petty irrelevancies by sceptics, yet such views, when properly examined, are emotionally based and lack intellectual credibility. For example, the fact that Christianity was spread all across Europe by the *Romans* of all people is, in itself, nothing short of miraculous and yet the Rationalists conveniently choose to ignore such blatant evidence of divine intervention.

The truth is that life without the supernatural is very dull indeed and the Western materialistic world is a world devoid of mystery, mysticism and the fantastical. People from all walks of life down the ages have been fascinated and captivated by magic, the occult, miracles and the unexplained mysteries and paradoxes that give rise to awe, reverence, and wonder, and provide richness to the fabric of our lives. The New Age movement, with its ghosts, angels, goddesses, fairies, witches, evil spirits and astrology, is arguably no more faddish and a product of our time than the dogmas of conventional science. Belief in the Big Bang theory has only existed since the 1960s, whereas a belief in the supernatural has been in existence since the inception of time. It is celebrated in all forms of art, drama, dance and music. Such rich diversity of art informed by the supernatural is too wonderful and culturally too all pervasive not to be treated more respectfully and mindfully by non-believers – it has been with us since the dawn of time.

All of this is relevant to our understanding of such practices as EFT. The mysterious, unexplained aspects of life must always be taken into consideration in the study of any subject that involves bringing about change in a living being, and this includes any attempts to heal a troubled mind and body. In order to understand and benefit from EFT, an open mind is essential. EFT operates in a different world to traditional science and its workings are essentially mysterious, possibly even mystical: there are more things in heaven and earth than were ever dreamt of in the philosophy of materialistic science!

Which brings us back to Rupert Sheldrake's dogma number ten: 'Mechanistic medicine is the only medicine that is efficacious. Complementary and alternative medicine is ineffective.' (Sheldrake 2012, p.8) The self-evident purpose of this book is to introduce the reader to a meridian-based, non-invasive technique that has a proven scientific track record and requires no legal or illegal drugs and no conventional Western doctor to prescribe it. Ancient Chinese meridian-based procedures like acupuncture were in the past similarly regarded by mainstream medical science as being at best pseudo-science and at worst nonsense. Thankfully, studious and credible scientific investigators such as Sheldrake and Lipton, and writer and researcher Robert Mcluhan, professionally and passionately continue to highlight the insubstantial nature of such views.

The two-minute energy test

One of the important points to bear in mind with energy work is that regular periods of time taken away from the hustle and bustle of life are important. Just as we need, from time to time, to recharge the battery of our mobile phone, we need to do the same with our minds and bodies. It helps us reinvigorate our spirits and regain contact with the essential life force, which is both empowering and energising. With this in mind, we shall take this opportunity to pause here for a couple of minutes to enter a place of quiet, calm reflection in order to re-energise. This is a healthy and moreover vital practice if we are to begin to comprehend and master EFT.

Exercise one: re-energising

We now invite you to close your eyes and take a few deep breaths in and out. While doing this, focus on your breathing. Do this for one to two minutes (or longer if you like). When you return to the here and now, have a stretch and possibly a yawn, gently roll your head one way and then slowly circle your head the other way. Then why not take a few sips of some filtered or mineral water from a clean polished glass and open a window, or go outside to take in some fresh air?

Exercise two: paying attention to energy flow

Perhaps you can now notice energy gently flowing through your body and mind; take a while now to observe this energy, to feel this life-giving energy streaming through you. As you connect with this energy, recognise how it feels and become conscious of it. This is the vital Qi energy that flows through all of life.

This ends our initial re-energising session. Hopefully you now feel calmer, more relaxed, focused, re-energised and ready to continue our study.

The introduction of acupuncture to the West

Although acupuncture has been practised in China for thousands of years, it was completely unknown in the West until relatively recently. The concepts of Qi energy and meridian channels were problematic for Western scientists, because such phenomena had never been identified within the narrower scope of their understanding of anatomy. The cause for Western scepticism is perhaps misplaced, given that acupuncture has a rich and ancient history in China where its methods have clearly been proved to be successful over many generations of application. Yet the reasons for such scepticism are deep rooted and are due to the fundamental differences between Eastern and Western culture and philosophy, which have already been highlighted in this book.

It was not until the 1970s that Chinese medicine was formally introduced to America where Western doctors for the first time witnessed clinical acupuncture. It is difficult to overestimate how shocking and disturbing this initially was to these doctors. For the first time in Western history, sharp needles were used as the only form of anaesthetic in American operating theatres. Needles appeared to remove rather than cause pain – a novel and unbelievable concept to Western minds!

Despite attempts by sceptical doctors to discredit acupuncture, the prevailing evidence for its efficacy was overwhelming and indisputable. Although American physicians, with their empirically based view of science, did not have the perceptual and cultural framework of the Chinese to draw upon to find adequate explanations of how acupuncture actually worked, acupuncture was found to be successful in practice. American doctors started visiting China to study acupuncture first hand with a mind to practising its methods back home.

Over recent decades, a vast amount of data has been collected to support the valid use of acupuncture. The West now has some knowledge of the effects of acupuncture, which validates the concepts underlying traditional Chinese medicine. Studies have been conducted using functional magnetic resonance imaging (MRI) and positron emission tomography (PET), which have shown a direct relationship between the points stimulated by acupuncture and the activation of certain areas of the brain that are connected to specific functions.

It is becoming more difficult for Western scientists to discredit meridian-based interventions such as acupuncture due to the weight of scientific evidence that is being accumulated to support them. The new technologies such as MRI and PET have demonstrated that Chinese medicine offers a workable and practical way of alleviating significant health challenges that conventional allopathic medicine has failed so far to deal with adequately.

Today there is an ever-growing volume of research to support the clinical use of acupuncture. Important institutions such as the World Health Organization (WHO) have stated that acupuncture is a viable, cost-efficient way of healing many human and animal diseases. The list below offers some of the contemporary clinical uses of acupuncture that have evidence-based data to support their validity:

- pain treatment
- treatment of wounds
- neurological disorders
- ophthalmological disorders
- treatment of cardiorespiratory disorders

- reproductive disorders

- gastrointestinal disorders.

Chinese therapies have not only offered viable, safe and cost-effective alternatives to Western medicine, they have also in actuality opened the door to more advanced and enlightened ways of healing. The new experimental environment that emerged during the 1960s and 1970s encouraged some Western practitioners to start creating their own versions of the ancient, noble medical practices of China and Asia. Arguably, it is the first time that Western medical innovations have sprung from Asian roots expressing themselves in the form of energy meridian interventions.

It is possibly an unprecedented moment in history where Western minds are making valid contributory inroads into the scientific field of traditional Asian energy healing. With the advent of these revolutionary changes have come new technologies like MRI imaging and PET scans, which have facilitated scientific validation of acupuncture as scientists are finally able to substantiate the existence of meridians that support Chinese energy concepts.

3

The Birth of Tapping
Goodheart, Diamond
and Callahan

The pioneering work of Dr John
Diamond and Dr George Goodheart

As we have seen in Chapter 1, acupuncture originated in
the East where it was developed to treat a wide range of
physical ailments. The traditional Chinese acupuncturists
did not originally practise with a view to helping people
with emotional problems. It was only when Western
doctors started studying acupuncture that a psychological
dimension began to be incorporated into its application.
The development of what could be described as emotional
acupuncture came into being with the work of practitioners
like Dr George Goodheart and Dr John Diamond MD.

One of the greatest biological breakthroughs of the
twentieth century was Goodheart's discovery that there is
an energetic connection and energetic relationship between
the major muscles and organs of the body. Goodheart was a
successful American chiropractor who studied acupuncture
in 1962. He had the vision to foresee how acupuncture could
be combined with his own chiropractic and developed a new
method, which he called applied kinesiology. Goodheart
created a precise way of ascertaining specific information
from the body by using muscle testing.

A key discovery of Goodheart's was that he was able to gain the same efficacious results of an acupuncture treatment without the use of needles, by applying manual pressure to the acupuncture points. Additionally, he found he achieved similar results by tapping on these points. This was clearly a major advancement in Western medical practice: suddenly it was possible for treatments that were originally developed in the East to be adapted in a way that made their application much easier and less intimidating for both Western doctor and their patient alike.

Diamond, an Australian psychiatrist, is one of the most important medical practitioners in developing meridian-based therapies in the West and is a pioneer of alternative and holistic medicine. He is arguably the founder of meridian-based therapies. Starting from his background in psychiatry, Diamond developed a more holistic approach towards healing by focusing on the totality of the patient. He epitomises the spirit of the New Age in his eclectic approach to healing that is grounded in the Eastern philosophical notions of interconnectedness, whereby the environment fundamentally affects the individual both positively and negatively. His substantial medical experience led him to conclude that there were a variety of ways to raise energy and that healing could be positively affected by the creative arts, especially music and painting. For many years he has used music to help raise the Life Energy of his patients.

In the 1970s, Diamond took Goodheart's process of tapping and incorporated it into his clinical procedures to create Behavioural Kinesiology. Building on Goodheart's discovery of the energy relationship between the body's muscles and organs, Diamond showed that there is an additional corresponding link to specific emotions. He termed this the Three Sides of the Triangle: Muscle, Organ and Emotion. He noted that both positive and negative emotions were connected to the meridian energy channels in the body and he began to study these in some depth, developing various subcategories of the emotions.

Another significant procedure that Diamond brought to his new methodology was the use of verbal affirmations. When the patient was having pressure applied to particular acupuncture points, they were required to make some kind of positive statement or to think about themselves during the process. This novel intervention paved the way for meridian-based therapies and energy psychology to be further developed and utilised in the West.

Tapping with Dr Roger Callahan: the inventor of the meridian tapping procedure

The work of Goodheart and Diamond has resulted in a considerable contribution to the development of what later became known as EFT. However, the person who is most significant in this story is without doubt Dr Roger Callahan, whose groundbreaking discoveries and unorthodox techniques were fundamental to the development of EFT. Without Callahan there would have been no EFT, for it is Callahan who invented the meridian tapping technique upon which all EFT is based. Callahan does not call his technique EFT and so it cannot be described as such, nevertheless, for all practical purposes it is very similar to what later became known as EFT.

Callahan's background is traditional clinical psychology; however, unlike most of his colleagues he also had a keen interest in a number of other disciplines and subjects, many of which have been discussed in the previous chapters. It was his ability to put together his knowledge of these apparently diverse subjects and combine them with his traditional psychotherapy work that led him to create an entirely new therapy technique, which he christened Thought Field Therapy (TFT).

TFT is the point at which all these varied subjects meet together like contributory streams converging to form a new river. Some of the major disciplines that TFT brings together include the following:

- quantum physics

- biology

- Eastern concepts of energy systems

- clinical psychology

- acupuncture therapy

- applied kinesiology.

TFT seeks to influence the subtle energy flows of the body by accessing the same energy meridians as the acupuncturist. The fundamental difference is that TFT does not use needles to affect the energy channels; instead it requires the meridian end points on the body to be tapped on by the fingers. Tapping on the end points of various meridians stimulates the flow of energy along the energy channels, thus restoring the body's natural energy flows to health and wellbeing once more.

In TFT, these points on the body need to be tapped on in a prescribed sequence, while at the same time focusing on the emotional problem that is being treated, a process that Callahan calls 'thought tuning'. In practical terms this means thinking about the emotional problem you wish to resolve at the same time as you carry out the tapping process. It must be stressed that this is an absolutely essential part of the TFT protocol – it simply does not work without it. This may of course be upsetting for the patient since thinking about the problem may induce the patient to experience the very emotional disturbance they are attempting to heal. Meridian-based protocols are unusual in that they invite and encourage the patient to focus their full attention on the negative feeling, for by re-experiencing the intensity of the emotional problem, it is then possible to tap it away and the emotional disturbance can be entirely removed in just a matter of minutes.

TFT was initially born out of Callahan's disillusionment with traditional therapy techniques. It was while working as a psychotherapist that Callahan started to become frustrated by how long it was taking to cure his patients of their problems. He realised that many patients seemed condemned to years of often painful therapy where they were required to repeatedly relive traumatic events from their lives. At the same time, only a small minority of them ever improved.

As a result of this frustration Callahan fell into the habit of continually learning about new techniques outside of his profession's traditional training in the hope of healing his patients more effectively, especially those suffering from anxiety and phobias. He was particularly interested in Eastern energy-based treatments and the work of Goodheart. By 1980, Callahan had studied the Chinese meridian system of acupuncture and Goodheart's applied kinesiology. The stage was now set for the greatest breakthrough ever made in the development of EFT, which occurred after a completely unplanned event took place with one of Callahan's phobia patients.

It was while working with one of his patients, a woman called Mary, that Callahan accidentally stumbled upon a way of tapping on the same meridian end points on the body that acupuncturists had been using for thousands of years. Callahan had been treating Mary for over a year with a variety of conventional therapy techniques without any success. Mary suffered from an extreme fear of water and

Callahan had tried all kinds of techniques on her, but she still could not even go near the swimming pool situated just outside his office and any contact with water would induce a panic attack in her.

One day Mary told Roger that every time she thought about water she could actually feel this fearful emotion in a specific place in her stomach. Callahan was by now familiar with the Chinese concepts of energy meridians and acupuncture, so he immediately knew that there was a spot below the eye that was the end point of the stomach meridian. He asked Mary to just tap on this point below the eye while thinking about her fear of water in the hope that it might possibly remove the unpleasant sensation in her stomach, never dreaming that this simple action would have such amazing implications for the future of therapy.

Callahan was astonished to find that after two minutes of tapping, Mary cried out excitedly that her fear of water had completely evaporated. Much to Callahan's dismay Mary, in a state of wild euphoria, suddenly ran outside to the swimming pool and began splashing water over her face. Roger was concerned because he knew Mary could not swim and he ran after her to stop her from falling into the pool, but when he saw her he realised that something genuinely remarkable had been achieved by the tapping.

That evening, in the middle of a thunderstorm, Mary drove out to the beach and slowly walked into the ocean without any fear. She was completely cured of her water phobia.

Callahan began experimenting with the tapping technique by trying it out on some of his other patients. Most of the time it did not work, but on the few occasions it did, the results were very powerful, just as with Mary. These extraordinary results contravened everything Callahan had been trained to believe in. He was conditioned by his professional background to believe that negative emotions were caused by such things as our past experiences, our mental processes, nervous systems and the brain itself. In other words, it was a materialistic hardware problem – a fault in the machine. Callahan's revolutionary discoveries made him realise that this was not the case at all.

Diamond had earlier realised that manipulating certain acupuncture points could affect the emotions as well as our physical state. It seems likely that Callahan knew about Diamond's work, although Callahan does not appear to acknowledge Diamond so we cannot confirm this. Whether or not Callahan was influenced by Diamond, his exploration of tapping on certain meridian points certainly does seem to be building on Diamond's original discovery.

Callahan started making extensive use of muscle testing in his innovative new treatment sessions, a method he had taken from applied kinesiology. Callahan found that with some of his patients, a series of points needed to be tapped in a specific sequence in order for the tapping to be effective. He discovered that particular types of emotional disorders required specific sequences of points to be tapped on in order for the tapping process to be successful. He created a form of muscle testing which he used as a diagnostic procedure to accurately identify the type of emotional disorder the patient was suffering from, an essential part of the TFT protocol. In developing this muscle testing procedure, Callahan has acknowledged the great debt he owes to the work of Goodheart. Callahan's diagnostic methodology was inspired by Goodheart's applied kinesiology, which Callahan admired immensely, calling it the greatest example of mind/body interaction he had ever seen.

Extensive research took the ever-curious Callahan down a number of widely divergent tracks of investigation, leading him to study a wide range of subjects in order to try and understand the miraculous changes that he was beginning to witness in his patients through the tapping procedure. Callahan began studying quantum physics in an attempt to understand how his patients seemed to undergo such sudden energy transformations during the tapping process.

As we have seen in the previous chapter, Einstein showed us that everything in the universe is made of energy with his equation $E = MC^2$ and quantum physics has proved that molecules are not solid at all, instead being made up of energy fields. We have also seen that scientists such as Lipton have applied these concepts to the biology of the body, whereby the body is viewed as consisting of energy fields and that our health is dependent upon how energy forces within the body interact with each other. This in turn is very closely related to the ancient Eastern concept of Qi energy – the life energy that controls the functioning of the body, another concept fundamental to TFT.

TFT is based on the idea that our thoughts and emotions are also forms of energy that reflect human consciousness and they are held inside fields, similar to Lipton's biological energy fields. These fields are called thought fields and they are the most important concept in TFT. In fact, the whole of TFT is based on the premise that thought is energy, just as mass is energy in Einstein's universe. These thought fields are very similar to many other fields identified in the world of quantum physics that contain within them information and memories. The information held within energy fields is called 'active information' in quantum physics and it is considered to be a form of energy – the so-called 'subtle' energy of Eastern science.

Callahan has isolated the source of all emotional disturbances as being what he calls a 'perturbation' in the thought field. In Callahan's theory, a perturbation contains 'active information' of a very specific type. It is this disturbance in the thought field that causes the person to experience negative emotions and that causes the body's natural energy flows to be impeded, thereby creating an imbalance in the energy system. In more practical terms, this means that the patient's on-going emotional distress is not caused by the original traumatic event itself. It is the perturbation that is creating all the disturbances in the body and it is this that needs to be dealt with. By tapping on the meridian points as prescribed by Callahan, the perturbation is isolated and eliminated from the thought field, while the memories of the trauma remain without causing any distress to the patient.

Callahan, then, has introduced the radical notion that it is not the traumatic experience itself, or even what the patient's thoughts are regarding the traumatic event, that is at the root of the negative emotion. Rather, it is the perturbation in the thought field that activates changes in the body that produces the negative emotion. For Callahan, the most significant psychological changes that take place for the patient are primarily achieved at the energy level: it is the energy system that creates the emotional problem and it is by manipulating the energy system that the negative emotion is removed. Callahan maintains that these emotional problems are not hard wired into the brain as some scientists think, and he endorses Sheldrake's assertion that memory is not stored within the brain; it is stored within the energy system. This is perhaps easier to understand today as we stream videos from the internet; it is no longer necessary to have a hard copy of a film in the form of a DVD, as it's all in the software – the invisible energy fields flowing around the body!

TFT then, is a non-invasive treatment, causing no physical discomfort to the patient and can be completed in a matter of minutes. By applying TFT, remarkably fast resolutions to emotional problems can be gained and, even in the case of more serious problems, the treatment can be successful after just a few sessions. Compared with traditional therapy, patients find this a refreshingly painless process, which produces immediate and often permanent relief from often-longstanding problems.

Sometimes TFT does not work immediately, and this is often due to a phenomenon Callahan calls Psychological Reversal. This is a polarity block in the body's energy system where a reversed energy flow prevents the treatment from working properly. It is caused by the self-sabotaging attitude of the patient, whose negative thinking prevents them from being healed. However, this can be quickly resolved by tapping on the karate chop point during the TFT session. According to Callahan, this will remove the energy flow disturbance that is preventing TFT from working effectively. The concept of Psychological Reversal is very important in TFT and the removal of it through the simple tapping procedure recommended by Callahan greatly enhances the effectiveness of the whole process and boosts the overall health and wellbeing of the patient considerably.

Another procedure integral to the TFT process is the judicious use of the SUD (Subjective Units of Distress) scale. The SUD scale is a widely used tool in the psychology profession and can be applied to any kind of problem that a patient may be suffering from, whether it is emotional or physical. It is used in TFT to measure the intensity of the emotion the patient is feeling with regard to the problem they are being treated for.

The SUD scale ranges from one to ten, where ten is the very worst that you could possibly feel and one is the point where the disturbance has been completely removed. It has been found that the use of some kind of numerical scale helps a patient clarify the level of emotion they are feeling in a way that verbal descriptions cannot do. Psychologists have invented numerous complex scales; however, for the purposes of TFT, a simple SUD scale is all that is required. As part of the TFT treatment patients are required to locate where they think they are on the SUD scale several times during the tapping process. This gives immediate feedback on the rate of progress that the patient is making and it helps determine what the next step should be in the treatment session.

Callahan went on to develop a precise system of treatment for every type of emotional problem that his patients suffered from. He created a set of individual, tailor-made recipes for each type of emotional disturbance that needed to be worked on. According to Callahan, there is a particular tapping sequence that must be applied for each type of emotional problem that exists. He called these tapping sequences 'algorithms' because they are similar to the concept of algorithms used in mathematics where an algorithm is defined as a kind of formula for the precise series of steps that need to be taken in order to solve a problem.

Each algorithm, then, has its own unique tapping sequence, which involves tapping on a combination of points chosen from the 12 major end points of the body's energy system. A unique algorithm exists for each type of emotional problem including trauma, anxiety, phobia, depression, anger, guilt and obsession. For some emotional disorders there is a basic algorithm and a more advanced algorithm that can be used. For example, when treating anxiety, there is a simple anxiety algorithm and a complex anxiety algorithm available. Similarly, when treating trauma, there is a simple trauma algorithm and a complex trauma algorithm to choose from.

Standard procedure requires starting with a simple recipe, and if this does not deal with the problem then it is necessary to move onto a complex algorithm. In addition, some emotional disorders have more than two alternatives. In the case of trauma for example, there are four algorithms: simple trauma algorithm, complex trauma algorithm, complex trauma with anger algorithm and complex trauma with guilt algorithm. All the algorithms use the same points on the body; they are just tapped on in a different order. The following major tapping points are common to all algorithms:

- eyebrow spot

- under the eye spot

- under the arm spot

- the two collarbone spots

- little finger spot

- index finger spot.

There is also an added complication to Callahan's algorithms that he has incorporated into the tapping procedure called the gamut series, which he considers to be of great importance. Callahan had learned from his studies of NLP (Neuro Linguistic Programming) that particular eye movements can influence a person's stress levels and memory retrieval. He then discovered that the position of the eye could display a hidden perturbation. He identified a tapping point located on the back of the hand, which he called the gamut point, which, when tapped on while simultaneously moving the eyes in a prescribed way, could immediately reduce or remove the perturbation entirely. He also had a keen interest in split-brain research, which provided evidence that you could stimulate the right side of the brain (the creative side) by simply humming a tune, and stimulate the left side of the brain (the mathematical side) by counting.

To give you a flavour of the procedures involved during a typical TFT session, let us take a look at the process involved for a couple of emotional problems. For the purposes of this demonstration we shall be applying Callahan's simple stress/ phobia algorithm (Callahan 2001). (All the sequences and steps detailed in this chapter are adapted from Callahan's excellent book, *Tapping the Healer Within*.)

The procedure shall be as follows (see Figure 3.1):

1. Tune the thought field: pick a simple problem such as feeling stressed.

2. Rate your stress level on the SUD scale: remember the scale ranges from one (no stress) to ten (full blown stress).

3. Tap the karate chop point 15 times.

4. Tap the under the eye spot seven times.

5. Tap the under the arm spot seven times.

6. Tap the collarbone spot seven times.

7. Rate your position on the SUD scale. If your score has gone down to one, you have successfully removed the problem. If your score is either the same as before, or reduced but not completely gone, then follow the 9 Gamut Procedure.

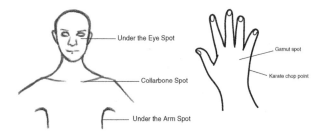

Figure 3.1: Head, body and hand

The 9 Gamut Procedure

The 9 Gamut Procedure is a sequence of nine quick steps that need to be carried out while simultaneously tapping the gamut spot on the back of the hand. The gamut spot can be found one inch below the knuckles and is situated between the little finger and the ring finger (see Figure 3.1). These steps can be done in any order. The nine actions are as follows:

1. Open eyes.

2. Close eyes.

3. Eyes point up and down to left.

4. Eyes point down right.

5. Roll eyes in one direction.

6. Roll eyes in opposite direction.

7. Hum a few notes of any tune.

8. Count from one to five.

9. Repeat the humming.

10. After completing the 9 Gamut Procedure, continue with the tapping procedure by repeating the same tapping sequence as before.

11. Tap the under the eye spot.

12. Tap the under the arm spot.

13. Tap the collarbone.

14. Rate your position on the SUD scale. If you are now down to one, then that's great – you have achieved your aim!

If you are still not fully comfortable, then you can further enhance your healing by following the collarbone/breathing exercise.

Collarbone/breathing exercise

This sequence may appear a little complicated to the layperson when encountering it for the first time. However, it is certainly well worth the time and effort it takes to master this exercise. The procedure is quite involved and challenging to remember. For this reason Callahan splits it into two practices; however, once fully grasped it is done as one single exercise.

PART ONE: THE BREATHING EXERCISE

This requires the following sequence to be carried out:

1. First, we are encouraged to breathe normally.

2. Then we take a full breath in and hold it.

3. We then let out half of that breath and hold the remaining half.

4. Then we let out the remainder of the breath and hold.

5. Finally, you take in a half breath and hold it.

This completes one round of the breathing exercise.

PART TWO: THE COLLARBONE TAPPING EXERCISE

This requires the following sequence to be carried out (see Figure 3.2):

1. Using either hand, place two fingers of one hand on one of the collarbone points and begin tapping,

while at the same time tapping the gamut position with the other hand's two fingers.

2. Move to the other collarbone and repeat the same sequence of tapping.

3. Move back to the original collarbone and form a fist on this point and begin tapping while continuing to tap the gamut point.

4. Return to the other collarbone point and continue to tap as above.

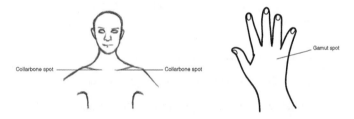

Figure 3.2 The collarbone/breathing exercise

This completes the first round. We now repeat the sequence from the beginning using the opposite hand.

1. Place two fingers on one of the collarbone points while tapping the gamut position with the other hand's two fingers and begin tapping the collarbone.

2. Move to the other collarbone and repeat the sequence of tapping.

3. Move back to the original collarbone and form a fist on this point and begin tapping, while continuing to tap the gamut point.

4. Return to the other collarbone point and continue to tap as above.

Once you are familiar with these steps then combine the breathing exercise with the collarbone tapping. After completing a full round of the collarbone/breathing exercise you will have completed 40 breathing and 40 tapping movements: 20 with the fingertips and 20 with the knuckles.

Authors' note: Callahan's collarbone/breathing exercise is a powerful way to help an anxious person to feel calm. The combination of breathing techniques, tapping processes, finger and fist swapping and counting is a substantial amount of information for the conscious mind to take in, keep track of and absorb. Additionally it is a fairly lengthy ritual. Experience has shown that this is a highly recommended practice.

The Apex Effect

The Apex Effect is an interesting problem highlighted by Callahan and one that he sometimes observed as a practitioner. When a person receives healing, particularly if it is miraculous or rapid in nature, it is common for the conscious mind to dismiss it as having nothing to do with the facilitator of the cure. We see this with spontaneous remissions of serious illnesses such as cancer. Doctors simply shrug their shoulders and cannot explain the dramatic change that has happened. There is a form of denial that takes place – the ego mind simply cannot accept it.

Sadly, this is not an uncommon phenomenon. It is experienced in other therapies such as hypnotherapy, where clients make incredible progress and then seem to forget they even had a problem in the first place. A trained practitioner will have experienced the Apex Effect in its many forms, and Callahan encountered it on numerous occasions. In Callahan's superb, must-read book *Tapping the Healer Within*

(2001), he recounts a fascinating story that goes something like this:

While he was attending the book launch of a well-known writer and acquaintance of his, Callahan bumped into the author outside the toilets just minutes before she was due to make a speech in a large room, crowded with expectant listeners. It was immediately clear to Callahan that the poor woman was absolutely terrified. The lady, who Callahan calls Kelly, suddenly blurted out, 'I would rather be thrown into a pool of killer sharks with all my bestseller books strapped to my legs than to have to go out there and make this talk', her whole body trembling as she spoke.

He was eager to try out his new TFT technique on her and she reluctantly agreed. There was barely enough time to do a couple of rounds of tapping before she had to make her dreaded speech. Callahan then keenly watched her walk into the room and mount the podium, wondering how she would cope. To his delight, Kelly was basking in a glow of warm confidence and proceeded to give a wonderful talk, wowing the audience with her personality, as if she had been making such speeches all her life. After the thunderous applause died down, Callahan approached Kelly, congratulating her on her performance. Almost as an aside, Callahan said he was so glad he was able to help her. She looked at him with astonishment and then with a wave of her hand said, 'Oh Roger, you haven't done anything at all!' (Callahan 2001, pp.7–10).

A favourite hypnotherapy tale goes like this. Once upon a time there was a lady called Phoebe who had a fear of heights. She booked a session with a local hypnotherapist who placed her subject into trance and made positive suggestions to remove the phobia. Phoebe thanked the practitioner and left the office with a spring in her step. One week later the therapist received a letter in the post from her client who wrote:

> Dear Diana it was lovely to meet you unfortunately the hypnosis didn't work – I heard every word you said, but as you were so nice I didn't want to point this out at the time. After our unsuccessful session together I gave myself a good talking to and decided I wasn't scared of heights after all. I then went to Paris for the weekend with my boyfriend and we climbed the Eiffel Tower! Yours, Phoebe.

Some might argue that this story points to the fact that the hypnotherapist may not have explained adequately to her client what hypnosis is all about and there perhaps could be some justification to this assertion. Nevertheless a form of the Apex Effect is certainly contained within this anecdotal account of rapid healing.

As an aside, it is interesting to note that the Apex Effect can take on many forms and is not just concerned with healing. Any form of benevolence can be conveniently forgotten. We are all very good at living in denial and this can take shape in many varied, surprising and even incredulous ways.

With regard to the principles of tapping, it is always a good idea to make notes of the severity of a person's original complaint and get them to participate in this process to help validate the Healing Event and reduce the risk of them experiencing the Apex Effect.

This concludes our main discussion of TFT as developed by Callahan. In the next chapter we will be looking at the work of Gary Craig, the founder of EFT, where it will become apparent just how crucial the work of Callahan has been in the evolution of tapping modalities.

4

The Emergence of EFT
The Work of Gary Craig

The development of EFT

EFT is an incredibly simple procedure that absolutely anyone can do. Once adequately explained, a five-year-old child could happily use EFT to good effect on herself, friends, family and pets. What's great about tapping is that you need little more than your fingertips and a body to tap on, and even these requirements are not strictly necessary as we shall discover later on.

We have already seen in Callahan's work on Thought Field Therapy (TFT) that this uses the same principles as acupuncture. It takes ancient Chinese concepts of energy and applies them in a new way by using an algorithmically prescribed tapping process whereby certain meridian points located on the body are tapped on sequentially in order to remove energy blockages and energy disturbances within the energy system.

EFT directly originates from TFT and it began when Gary Craig, a pupil of Callahan, radically refined Callahan's tapping procedure. Craig was an unusual student for Callahan in that his background was in engineering. However, Craig describes his young self as a sports enthusiast who went to Stanford University to study sports such as American football. As Gary himself admits, he was never going to become a professional sportsman, so he became interested in pursuing engineering as a career. Nevertheless, his fascination for all things sport-related led him to realise that his mind, particularly the thoughts he was thinking, had a direct relationship on how well he played on the day. This gave him a penchant for self-study in the areas of psychology and New Age philosophy and spirituality, motivating him to take various courses and to read avidly on a wide range of these subjects.

In this respect he was one of the first to support the egalitarian view that psychology, spirituality and healing should be brought into the public domain. In hindsight, this is surely one of Craig's greatest achievements: bringing EFT to us all and making it freely accessible to the whole world. Moreover, this clearly supports the spirit of the New Age and the 1960s notion that we can all be healers; we can all learn to support and play a significant role in the rising of consciousness of our planet.

Craig was probably the only trainee under Callahan who came from a non-therapy environment. Most of Callahan's pupils were from medical backgrounds in the form of doctors and psychiatrists. Craig represents a radical departure from the prevailing outlook of meridian-based practitioners at this time. He helped change perceptions of what kind of people healers could be, introducing the notion that one does not need to be a doctor to effectively help people with emotional problems. This, of course, is further reinforced today through the educational tool of the internet where these hierarchical and elitist structures are further being challenged and replaced by a more democratic appreciation of sharing and disseminating information in a caring and unselfish manner. Craig's freely available EFT certainly embodies this loving and giving attitude.

Callahan, to his credit, encouraged Craig in his studies and considered it healthy and refreshing to have a layperson's perspective. This was both insightful and intuitive of Callahan, and his acceptance of Craig was soon to be rewarded, as the EFT founder became Callahan's star pupil.

One of the objections to Callahan's model was that it was overly complex, which made it difficult to learn, and it was primarily effective only with the guidance of a highly trained therapist. Craig's genius was to make tapping an incredibly simple procedure that absolutely anyone can do. Craig's experiences with tapping led him to the discovery that it was generally not necessary to tap in any particular order or sequence for the treatment to be effective or for outstanding results to take place. Just tapping the same meridian points on each patient was all that was required to deal with the majority of emotional problems and in 1994 Craig developed a simplified tapping procedure that he named EFT (Emotional Freedom Techniques).

Undoubtedly, Craig's outstanding achievement and contribution to energy healing psychology was to dramatically simplify Callahan's TFT process and make it accessible to lay people as well as therapists. Additionally, Craig maintains that one of the fundamental differences between EFT and traditional psychotherapy is that it is not necessary in EFT to focus excessively on past unpleasant memories or traumas. Indeed this is considered to be unhelpful because it may recreate unnecessary distress and pain. EFT deals with energy disturbances rather than memories – this is a very significant distinction.

The underlying principles of Craig's Emotional Freedom Techniques (EFT)

Craig has developed what he calls the 'Discovery Statement', which says that 'the cause of all negative emotions is a disruption in the body's energy system' (Craig 2011). He goes on to explain that these energy disturbances are akin to a malfunctioning TV set, where the picture and sound are distorted by energy disruptions. Craig further elaborates that if no energy disturbance in the energy body has taken place, there will be no evidence of a negative emotional problem.

This idea that all emotional problems have the same cause has far-reaching implications: it means that the same general procedure can be used to remove all emotional issues. Moreover, it becomes self-evident that a person who talks of an emotional problem must have an energetic imbalance. This is significant because it implies that we can greatly simplify the diagnostic process. The reader may already have gleaned that this is a major departure from Callahan's TFT procedure where correct diagnosis is seen as paramount and a prerequisite to offering a healing protocol.

Nevertheless, it would be erroneous to conclude from this that the competent EFT practitioner is incapable of, or sees no need for, the skilful application of sophisticated diagnostic methods when conducting EFT; indeed this is what sets the professional apart from the amateur. Rather, we can state here that for a wide range of emotional conditions and situations, the overly complex Callahan methodology is superfluous and deemed largely irrelevant. It could even be seen as an elaborate overindulgence on behalf of the practitioner.

Perhaps a simple engineering example here may help us to understand better these distinctions. If we have a bicycle and we need to put some air into its tyres, then why use expensive sophisticated air pressure machines found in petrol stations when often all that is needed is a manual hand pump? Obviously these machines are extremely useful for inflating large vehicles' tyres and equally helpful for bicycles with serious tyre deflations, but why use them when a simple solution is at hand in the form of a bicycle pump? We could extend this metaphor by saying that one of the skills of the expert is to choose the appropriate tools for the job. In this case, a portable hand pump is the correct, sensible and elegant choice, even allowing the job to be carried out by a child, with no necessity of a trained mechanic overseeing the process.

This is where Craig's practical engineering background has been an immensely positive influence on his attitudes towards healing. Craig is someone who is looking for simple solutions that work in the real world. EFT, just like the bicycle pump and the child who pumps it, requires little training or expertise and in the majority of cases it simply works!

It will now be clear to the reader that EFT takes ancient Chinese concepts of energy and acupuncture and applies them in a new way without the use of needles. It accommodates a simple tapping process whereby certain meridian end points located on the body are tapped on to remove energy blockages and energy disturbances within the energy system, thus improving energy flow and smoothing out energy imbalances.

As we have already stated, EFT is an incredibly simple procedure that absolutely anyone can do: once it was adequately explained to them, a five-year-old child could happily use EFT to good effect on herself, family and pets. So now let's take a look at the components of the EFT process, so that you can immediately begin to get a feel for how amazing this technique can be in your hands with the minimum of help and guidance. It is well worth repeating here that in order to practise EFT you need little more than your fingertips and a body to tap on, and even these requirements are not strictly necessary as we shall discover later on.

The original Craig EFT 'recipe'

Craig compares the EFT process to baking a cake, and EFT has four ingredients that need to be in place for the recipe to be successful. The basic recipe is as follows:

1. the Set Up

2. the Sequence

3. the 9 Gamut Procedure

4. return to the Sequence.

1. The Set Up

The Set Up could be considered to be one of the most important elements of EFT. Without the Set Up there is no real EFT. It is called the Set Up because we are 'setting up' the energy system in order for the tapping process to work. According to Craig, the energy system is an intricate network of electrical circuits and we have to ensure that the energy system is correctly set up before we can remove any energy disturbances when we begin tapping.

Before any EFT session can commence, you need a reason to tap and this is where the ingenuity of the Set Up becomes immediately apparent. The good news is you can tap on any subject you like – it is infinitely flexible and may cover the entire spectrum of human experience. Craig enthusiastically suggests we 'try it on anything!' Whatever you want to change, work on, improve, or, as Energists like to put it, 'evolve', is encapsulated within the Set Up.

To gain outstanding results, the Set Up needs to be carefully considered and skilfully crafted, for the correct Set Up is akin to the golden key that unlocks the door – the 'Open, Sesame' heralding a new dawn. To put it less poetically: when you get the Set Up right you are well on your way to a Healing Event and that is a wonderful and remarkable achievement!

THE SET UP IN PRACTICE

First, we name the presenting problem, or issue, and form a simple sentence that sums up this particular problem. For example, take a person who has a fear of lifts/elevators. They may say out loud three times: 'Even though I have a fear of lifts/elevators, I deeply and completely love and accept myself'. This would take place while the client rubs the 'sore spot' (collarbone position) or taps on the karate chop point.

It is important to notice that within the Set Up sentence, two important requirements are being satisfied:

1. The client vocalises their problem.

2. Despite this negative expression of the problem, the client states quite categorically that, at a deep level at least, they love and accept themselves.

Craig insists that, although it is not necessary for the client to actually believe the Set Up sentence to be true for the affirmation to be appropriate, expressing the sentence with full conviction is helpful and preferable.

While the tapping is in process, the client is required to focus their attention completely on the energy disturbance, therefore an abbreviated phrase that sums up the Set Up sentence is repeated during the tapping round. This shortened statement is known as the reminder phrase. So in our example, the full sentence, 'Even though I have a fear of lifts/elevators, I deeply and completely love and accept myself', could be shortened to: 'fear of lifts/elevators', and this would form the reminder phrase. The reason for reducing the length of sentence is so the client can fully concentrate on the problem while conducting the EFT round.

2. The Sequence

This involves tapping the end points of the major energy meridians. These are the same acupressure points identified from acupuncture. This tapping procedure removes the energy disturbances and restores harmony and balance to the energy system. Craig recommends tapping these points about seven times each. All the energy meridians used in EFT have two end points; however, we only need to tap on one of these ends to correct the energy flow. We use the points that are situated near the surface of the body, as these are easier to reach.

Before introducing the original tapping points of EFT in order of sequence, we would like to explain here that, because of the natural symmetry of the body, you can use either side of the body to tap the points, and it makes no difference which side you choose. It is also perfectly acceptable to swap from one side to the other during the tapping procedure – it makes no difference to the outcome of the EFT session.

The tapping points are as follows (see Figure 4.1):

1. *Tapping point one*: eyebrow point (EB).

2. *Tapping point two*: the side of the eye (SE).

3. *Tapping point three*: under the eye (UE).

4. *Tapping point four*: under the nose (UN).

5. *Tapping point five*: the chin (CH).

6. *Tapping point six*: collarbone (CB).

7. *Tapping point seven*: under the arm (UA).

8. *Tapping point eight*: the hand sequence: starting with the outside edge of the thumb, systematically tap each finger, omitting the ring finger.

9. *Tapping point nine*: finish with the karate chop point (KC).

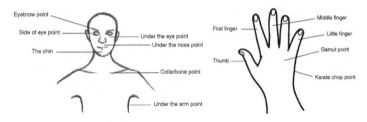

Figure 4.1 Tapping points

3. The 9 Gamut Procedure

Authors' note: although this is classic Callahan and his original version has been described in the previous chapter, Craig's version of the procedure is detailed here as well. In later versions of EFT, the 9 Gamut Procedure is not so much omitted as sidelined because of its rather quirky characteristics. However, it must be stated that although arguably it is not necessary in the majority of basic EFT interventions, it can be extremely useful in certain circumstances. It has been included in this section because it was used by Craig in his basic recipe of EFT and certainly was considered an important function at that time. Incidentally, disciples of Callahan today still place much emphasis on the 9 Gamut Procedure.

Although it might seem as if EFT has lost the plot at this stage, stay with us – it's all good fun! The 9 Gamut Procedure is as follows:

First, locate the gamut (triple burner) point: this is located on the back of the hand below the gap between the little finger and the ring finger (see Figure 4.1).

This gamut point is then tapped continually while carrying out the following steps:

1. Eyes closed.

2. Eyes open.

3. Eyes hard down right (keep head steady).

4. Eyes hard down left (keep head steady).

5. Roll eyes all the way round in one direction.

6. Roll eyes round in opposite direction.

7. Hum a few notes of a song such as 'Happy Birthday'.

8. Count rapidly from one to five.

9. Repeat 'Happy Birthday' again for a few seconds.

This concludes the 9 Gamut Procedure.

4. Return to the Sequence

This involves directly repeating the Sequence, which begins with tapping the eyebrow points (EB) and ends with tapping the karate chop point (KC). This concludes a basic round of EFT treatment.

Further rounds of EFT

It is the hope and heartfelt desire of every EFT practitioner to eradicate the presented problem in a single EFT round. It's wonderful when this takes place – a truly exhilarating feeling, similar to winning the jackpot, hitting the bull's eye or scoring a hole in one in golf! Moreover, removing a problem with a single round of EFT is far more frequent and likely than these examples may indicate. In fact, it is this regular achievement that sets EFT apart from traditional medical practice. Complete healing with a single, one-minute EFT treatment is a fairly common experience, whereas in traditional medicine, such rapid success would be the exception not the norm.

Sometimes, however, one round of tapping is not enough to completely remove the disturbance. In this case, further rounds of tapping are required. Before further rounds of EFT are embarked upon, it is necessary to adjust the Set Up statement so that it accurately reflects where the client currently is in terms of the shifting emotions surrounding the presenting issue.

A simple example here may serve to describe this refinement. Let us imagine that your friend Janet has got a severe headache and comes to you for a bit of EFT help. The original Set Up sentence could be: 'Even though I have this thumping headache, I totally love and accept myself.' The reminder phrase could be: 'thumping headache'. After the first EFT round she feels considerably better, yet there is still a residue of discomfort remaining. The new Set Up sentence could be: 'Even though there is still a bit of pain remaining in my head, I totally love and accept myself.' The reminder phrase could be changed to: 'little bit of pain'. The next EFT round takes place with an assessment at its completion that finds Janet's headache completely gone.

Generally speaking, EFT rounds continue and Set Up phrases and reminder phrases are further refined, until the problem is either resolved or the session needs to be continued at another time.

The marvels of the SUD scale

When EFT was first designed by Craig, he adapted Callahan's measurement scale that had already been in wide use by medical doctors and psychologists. We have already seen that this was known as the SUD scale (Subjective Units of Discomfort) and was used to measure the amount of pain a patient felt. Craig's scale ranges from zero to ten where ten is the most uncomfortable a client can feel and zero is the point when the problem has completely gone.

The use of the SUD scale in EFT is similar to its application in Callahan's TFT: it enables the client and the therapist to gain a subjective insight into the intensity of the presenting emotional problem at any given time. If a client has no present negative emotional charge then EFT cannot be administered – there would be little point. This is where the SUD scale is very useful. At the start of each EFT round, it is normal procedure to ask the clients to state where they would place themselves on the scale. This helps to test the strength of the emotional response and subsequently to measure the intensity and progress after each EFT round.

For EFT to work effectively, it is necessary for the client to experience the negative emotion sufficiently for it to be removed. The aim of EFT therefore is often to try and increase the negative response to as high a level as possible so as to reduce the emotional disturbance and free the client of the issue completely. In this respect, EFT is unusual as a therapeutic modality in that it not only focuses on negativity, but it also actually requires the client to experience as high a level of emotional intensity as possible. As we have said, this is necessary to deal completely with the emotional condition being treated or at least to substantially reduce the unpleasant energetic disturbance.

The SUD scale helps to measure the success of the EFT treatment. EFT can be seen to be working when the client is experiencing positive shifts and changes, and the SUD scale can show these subjective, incremental changes that are taking place. This can be a valuable tool to both therapist and client throughout the EFT treatment. Using Craig's scale, once the client has reached zero, this indicates that a complete healing has taken place.

Here is a simple, light-hearted example of the SUD scale at work. You are angry with your cat, as it hissed and spat at you because you had refused to give it a piece of your kipper fillet. While you were shouting and cussing, it bit your leg and ran off before you could grab it (the cat that is!). You decide to do some self-help EFT (on you and the cat) and note that the angry feeling in your stomach and the pain in your leg equate to ten on the SUD scale.

Your Set Up phrase is: 'Even though I am livid with my cat, I totally love and accept myself.' The reminder phrase is: 'livid!' Your first round of tapping leaves you feeling no longer livid but mildly irritated, with the leg pain gone. You take another SUD scale reading and you estimate a measurement of three. Your next round Set Up phrase could be: 'Even though some anger remains in the form of mild irritation, I totally and completely love and accept myself.' The reminder phrase is now: 'mild irritation'. After tapping this round of EFT you burst out laughing; all the anger has subsided and you are expressing warm loving, forgiving feelings towards your cat. Success! A zero on the SUD scale is measured. Well done.

Additional considerations

Craig says that one of the greatest errors newcomers to EFT make is that they tap on problems that are too general. For example, people say things such as: 'I hate myself, I am a complete failure!', 'I'm no good at maths!', 'All men/ women are pigs'. or 'Nobody likes me. I'm unattractive to the opposite sex.' While it is certainly okay to tap on these global statements, in all likelihood you will simply tap away the stress underlying these statements and little else. (Although reducing stress is in itself extremely useful, as you will discover later in the book.)

Be specific!

Although EFT works well on general affirmations such as: anger, fear, worry, loss of confidence, etc., it is always a good idea to be specific. If a person says they feel depressed or unhappy, it is possible to remove this emotion; however the more specific you can be, the better. When trapeze artist and circus owner Richard West visited an EFT practitioner he was in despair. It was only later in the session that the real reason why he had sought help was revealed: he had a lifelong, crippling shyness around the opposite sex – particularly those he found attractive. The problem was exacerbated because professionally he was constantly surrounded by dancers and other glamorous performers and entertainers.

As soon as he nervously came through the door and shook the therapist's hand he immediately slumped in a chair holding his hands in his head. Richard then spat out: 'Everyone thinks I've got it made, but it's all one huge pretence. The sad fact is I'm a born failure.'

Richard's extreme emotional outpouring was an indication to the practitioner of the need for a round or two of EFT to remove Richard's stress before she could begin to ascertain the real nature of the problem. After a warm-up round of EFT, Richard was calm enough to explain he felt uncomfortable around women. By tapping on 'uncomfortable around women', he became even more specific and admitted that it was only women in social situations he felt troubled by. The session played out as follows:

By the end of the second round, Richard had noticeably brightened and a smile had emerged on his face. 'Okay,' he stated, 'I am a brilliant entertainer and a pretty good entrepreneur. It's just that I've never been much good with women in clubs and bars.'

By careful questioning the therapist was able to tease out of her client the precise reason for his anxiety. Richard admitted: 'I just turn to jelly when I'm trying to ask a girl for a date.' The next treatment round of EFT had the Set Up: 'Even though I turn to jelly when trying to get a date, I totally and completely love and accept myself.' And this successfully dealt with Richard's lifelong angst around beautiful women he was attracted to and plucking up the courage to ask them out.

This EFT story highlights the benefits of being as specific as possible, while dealing with emotional problems, such as the one faced by our circus entertainer, Richard.

Psychological Reversal and Secondary Gain

EFT can, and often does, remove problems rapidly. Conversely, from time to time, it is possible that EFT can appear not to be working so well. There may be many reasons for this. Two causes in particular are worth looking for: Psychological Reversal and Secondary Gain.

One frequent impediment to the success of EFT is said to be the effect of Psychological Reversal (PR), a phenomenon that also arises in TFT (see Chapter 3). PR highlights a significant challenge for practitioners when they appear to encounter resistance to healing from the client or patient. This could be obvious resistance or be more subtle in the form of an unconscious response.

PR occurs when the energy flow is disturbed and begins to move in the wrong direction. This is known as a polarity reversal and is caused by negative thinking. This may be in addition to the negative emotion being explored by the EFT round and could interfere with the EFT session, possibly preventing EFT from being effective. It is therefore important to deal with this reversal. Fortunately, Craig's basic EFT recipe contains within it a simple tapping process to correct this reversal: just tap on the karate chop point a number of times.

Secondary Gain also describes a situation where a client is resistant to the healing process. However, in the case of Secondary Gain, the individual has quite rational reasons for why they don't actually want to get better. Let us take a hypothetical example to explain how Secondary Gain works.

Justin (an imaginary person) has a bad back and has been out of work for three years. He no longer has to get up at 6.00am in the morning, take the dog out in the rain, ferry the kids to school, help his wife with the daily chores and put the garbage out. Obviously, it's not an ideal life and there are parts of it that he misses; however, his boss has been very generous to him and continues to keep him as an employee on full pay. His wife and children have been fully supportive and overall it could be a lot worse. Justin has a wry sense of humour and jokes about it this way: 'Well I don't like having backache; but it sure beats work any day. A bad day at home is far better than a good day at the office.' There are many reasons why Justin prefers to stay sick!

Justin's attitude is by no means an exception. You probably know or have encountered one or two people like Justin. It is a commonplace occurrence in life and has probably been taking place throughout history. Indeed, there is a fascinating case of Secondary Gain to be found in the Bible. In the New Testament Gospel of John there is a story told about Jesus in which he is introduced to a man who had been an invalid for 38 years at the side of the Pool of Bethesda. Apparently this pool was well known for its miraculous healing powers, when an angel of the Lord would daily stir its waters to energise its potency. Folk in need of healing from far and wide flocked in droves to get into the pool to receive an instant cure. Often the sick would need to queue due to the immense popularity of this much-welcomed resource. As the miraculous healing occurred but once a day, demand far exceeded supply! When Jesus met the invalid, remarkably he asked him: 'Do you want to get well?' It could be that Jesus found it curious that a person would still be hanging around for so long without taking the plunge! What was stopping him?

This scripture indicates that Secondary Gain has been around for thousands of years and was something that the 'Great Physician' was well familiar with and capable of dealing with when appropriate!

Components

Sometimes, problems are complex and have a number of 'aspects' to them. Each of these parts needs to be tapped on separately in order to bring about a complete removal of the issue. For example, if a person has a fear of speaking in public, there may be many components to such a condition: they may be afraid of crowds; the type of lights; the location of the venue and whether it's indoors or outdoors; the time of day; the time of year, etc.

The components of a problem can therefore be any number of things. It is the skill of the enquirer to discover, through appropriate questioning of the client, what those components are and then to use EFT on each one individually until the problem is dealt with. If a person has a fear of spiders, they must isolate exactly what it is about the spider that they are afraid of. A series of questions can help identify this: 'What is it particularly about the spider you don't like?' The client could respond that they don't like their beady eyes, and their creepy long hairy legs or the speed and the manner they crawl around, lurking in the shadows, waiting behind every corner!

This may appear to the reader to be a daunting prospect and somewhat beyond the layperson's ability. The general guideline is: only deal with issues that you feel capable of handling. If a simple few EFT rounds do not resolve the problem, then this could be an indication of a complex issue and it may be necessary or advisable to contact a professional EFT practitioner.

Craig's Generalisation Effect

Craig has identified a phenomenon that he calls Generalisation, which has a very positive effect on the outcome of certain problems that EFT seeks to resolve. Craig's 'Generalisation Effect' can be explained as follows. If you have a number of related issues that need to be tapped on, beginning to resolve a few of those issues can result in collapsing the remaining associated issues. This is similar to the domino effect, where once a few dominoes begin to fall, they topple other dominoes next in line until the entire sequence of dominoes quickly fall down.

This can obviously be of great practical benefit, and an understanding of the Generalisation Effect has many uses. It is one of the reasons why a sequential approach to administrating EFT, and tapping on component parts of a problem in a particular order, can be the best method to deal with complex challenges.

Let's imagine that there is a dear friend of yours called Eileen who unexpectedly knocks on your dormitory door at 3.00am one Monday morning in a very emotional and agitated state. She has clearly been crying heavily throughout the night – black mascara is running from her eyes and her ruby red lipstick is smudged across her face.

'Eileen, whatever is the matter?' you ask.

Eileen immediately begins gabbling: 'Oh I'm at my wit's end – I know I'm going to fail all my assignments miserably. I haven't had a wink of sleep since Saturday and I've got an important exam tomorrow, which I haven't revised for. To make things worse, I had a blazing row last night with my boyfriend, Tom, who has threatened to leave me, all my friends are sick of me because I keep moaning all the time and I'm in a right mess. Help!'

You invite her in and make a pot of tea while Eileen goes to the bathroom to clean herself up and make herself respectable. Your first round of EFT focusing on her study woes dramatically removes a lot of the emotional intensity that Eileen has been feeling and amazingly she says she now feels 100 per cent able to do well in her test tomorrow. What is perhaps even more surprising is that this new feeling of confidence seems to have generalised into other areas of her life. She says she is now looking forward to putting the past behind her and making it up with her friends.

You now tap on 'the argument with Tom' and this brings a profound shift of warm loving feelings towards her estranged boyfriend. Eileen's attitude seems to be well on the way to being completely transformed. You go to make another cup of tea and when you return five minutes later, you find your friend contentedly curled up on your sofa sleeping like a baby, her apparent sleep problem successfully dealt with.

The following afternoon, you receive another knock on the door and a beaming Eileen presents you with a huge bunch of white carnations and invites you to a slap-up meal along with her, Tom and the rest of her friends.

This concludes our discussion of Craig's EFT basic recipe.

Basic EFT practice exercise

- Pick a memory that makes you feel a little uncomfortable.

- Rate this feeling on the SUD scale from zero to ten (ten being very uncomfortable).

- Now verbally describe your feeling (the Set Up phrase) and rub the sore spot or tap the karate chop position as you say out loud your affirmation.

- Now shorten this sentence with a key word or phrase that sums up the sentence (the reminder phrase).

- Now begin to tap, starting at the eyebrow, and working down the body through all the tapping points, until you complete the Sequence part of the basic EFT recipe,

- Now have a go at the 9 Gamut Procedure (good luck!).

- Finish by repeating the Sequence, stopping once you have tapped the karate chop position.

Congratulations, you have now completed your first round of EFT!

Now check how much the problem has been removed. You can use the SUD scale if you like. If the issue has vanished, pat yourself on the back – you have witnessed how powerful a one-minute round of EFT can be! If there is still a little of the problem left, conduct another round or two until the problem is resolved. Remember to modify your Set Up and reminder phrases after each round and regularly test yourself with the SUD scale throughout the EFT session.

This provides a clear outline of the basic EFT protocol and contains all the ingredients you need to get you started on doing EFT on yourself and others.

A practical tip for mastering the basic EFT protocol
To conclude the basic EFT protocol, we would like to offer you the following advice. As there is a substantial amount of information in this content-rich chapter, we highly

recommend that you reread it several times so as to fully absorb the principles of Craig's EFT.

In the following chapter, we will explore the development of EFT and see what we can do to enhance the basic EFT recipe and how it can be used in exciting ways beyond removing remedial problems.

5

The Evolution of EFT
From Craig to Hartmann

Although Craig's EFT clearly stems from Eastern energy concepts and comes directly from Callahan's TFT, in many ways it was seen at its inception as being something entirely original and new – a healing modality that was wonderfully powerful and refreshingly novel both at the same time. Two things set EFT apart in the minds of those early EFT enthusiasts. First, that it was so incredibly easy to do. Once it was properly explained to them, nearly anybody could apply EFT and get impressive results almost immediately. This was especially liberating and placed therapy for the first time in the hands of non-medical folk. Second, the power and efficacy of this simple tapping procedure became immediately apparent to all who experienced it. It literally blew the proverbial socks off anything that had preceded it. For the first time ever, simple yet profoundly fast healing was possible and Craig had put EFT directly in the hands of the layperson.

This surely was Craig and EFT's greatest achievement. Now it was no longer necessary for an emotionally unwell person to have prolonged and disturbing treatment sessions with a doctor or psychiatrist who, despite their rigorous academic and professional training and best intentions, was more often than not unable to bring about cure – certainly not such a rapid cure as EFT could bring to ordinary people.

Indeed, witnessing speedy recovery was a regular event for those early EFTers, rather than the exception. Moreover, what is also truly amazing about EFT (and lifesaving at times) is its ability to repeatedly remove long-term emotional problems in a matter of seconds! Little wonder that the New Age healing community was so excited and began vibrating with energetic enthusiasm for this 'new kid on the block' energy tapping technique. Finally, a medical, philosophical and healing synthesis of Eastern and Western minds and traditions had given birth to something rather exceptional: EFT! It was the start of a new era, as the arrival of EFT brought with it, and in turn was itself swept along by, an upsurge in the rising tide of energy healing awareness and grassroots participation, and it was the secret hope of the father of EFT that this would, in the long term, bring about an increase and raising of spiritual consciousness on our entire planet (more on this fascinating insight later).

Although EFT was at this time naturally in its infancy, it was developing quickly and it soon began to outgrow its infant garments – the basic EFT recipe that Craig had initially clothed it in. EFT was maturing fast. It may be expedient at this juncture to invite the reader to join us in taking a closer look at exactly what some of those innovations were, and how this exciting new healing phenomenon fared over the passage of time to the place where it nobly stands today, in the hope that it may shed sufficient light on the subject to allow those of us who are keen to get a real handle on EFT to begin to appreciate just how divergent its techniques have become. Interestingly, these innovations may or may not be deemed relevant to the individual EFT practitioner; one of the nice things about the evolving EFT is that there is plenty of room for the uniqueness of the individual to be expressed within both EFT's practice and administration.

In this chapter we will highlight a few of Craig's revisions and attempt to suggest that, despite some minor alterations, EFT has indeed evolved; however, not so much in terms of technical advancement. Rather, it has developed in terms of its wider goals, objectives and initiatives, which since the start have been growing ever confidently towards a more positive and spiritually orientated direction, instead of staying rigidly stuck in the remedial meridian-based tapping mindset of the pre-EFT early days and environments that EFT sprang from.

The new, improved Craig EFT recipe

The good news is that although Gary's original EFT recipe has changed little since its inception, EFT has nevertheless improved and has become even easier to use. As the saying goes: 'Less is often more.' Craig's revisions of early EFT not only make EFT even simpler, they also cut out some of the more arduous time-consuming tapping processes, making an EFT round even faster than the nifty original recipe. With shortcuts like the removal of the 9 Gamut Procedure and thumb and finger positions, you can experience an EFT round even more rapidly than before.

Table 5.1 details exactly what these changes are, so that you can begin to have fun with EFT and experience for yourselves just how useful and significant these refinements could be for you while using EFT on yourself, a family member, a colleague, a loved one, a friend or even a pet.

TABLE 5.1 DIFFERENCES BETWEEN CRAIG'S ORIGINAL EFT RECIPE AND MODERN EFT RECIPE

Procedure	Craig's original EFT recipe	Craig's modern EFT recipe
The Set Up[1]	Rub the sore spot (collarbone)	Rub the karate chop point
The tapping points:		
Top of head	Omitted	Tapped
Eyebrow	Tapped	Tapped
Side of eye	Tapped	Tapped
Under eye	Tapped	Tapped
Under nose	Tapped	Tapped
Chin	Tapped	Tapped
Collarbone	Tapped	Tapped
Under arm	Tapped	Tapped
Thumb	Tapped	Omitted
Fingers (no ring finger)	Tapped	Omitted
The 9 Gamut Procedure	Carried out	Omitted

[1]This is just a minor adjustment to the Set Up procedure (actually, in Craig's original EFT recipe, both the sore spot and the karate chop point were allowed; however, Craig suggested the sore spot was slightly more effective in the majority of cases. The modern EFT recipe removes the sore spot entirely and replaces it with the karate chop point).

NOTES

- It can be seen that the modern Craig EFT recipe introduces Callahan's top of head point (see Figure 5.1) as the first tapping point and he omits the thumb and finger positions as well as the 9 Gamut Procedure.

- Although Gary has now omitted the 9 Gamut Procedure, he is not saying it is ineffective, yet he would suggest it wasn't necessary in the majority of cases.

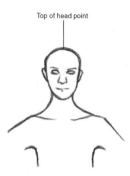

Figure 5.1 Callahan's top of head point

A note on the many variations of EFT

EFT has spawned a variety of variations on the theme of Craig's original EFT protocol. Practitioners have tended to tailor their sessions around their own preferences and favourite ways of conducting EFT. This is a fairly natural outcome of the evolving democratic, organic nature of the EFT process. Craig's laidback attitude to what could be called the 'all inclusive non-restrictive openness' of EFT certainly has inspired unique approaches to this fascinating modern tapping modality. Simply put: 'Anything goes!'

EFT has creative impetus built within it – a non-standardised laissez-faire approach that helps keep EFT fresh, vibrant, spontaneous and ever-evolving. You are similarly encouraged to experiment with EFT and see what best works for you and those you practise on. With this in mind, we concentrate on the three most important and popular tapping methods on offer – Callahan's TFT, Craig's EFT and Hartman's EnergyEFT – because there is a wealth of EFT resources contained within the extensive body of these disciplines, rather than bogging the reader down in a mire of EFT distractions through an intense and unnecessary analysis of these many EFT forms.

Authors' note: We encourage the reader always to act responsibly. As Craig says: 'Don't go where you're not confident!' – meaning if that EFT does not appear to be getting positive results for you and your patient, it is recommended that you seek professional guidance.

EFT has been safely used by thousands of people all over the world for the last 20 years or so and it is extremely rare that there are negative repercussions from using EFT – the worst that could possibly happen is nothing takes place at all or that one ends up with a headache from overzealous tapping!

Moving away from the negative (remedial problems) to the positive: an introduction to Dr Silvia Hartmann

Meridian-based therapies such as Callahan's TFT and Craig's original EFT aimed to remove emotional problems. Nevertheless, the evolution of EFT is clearly moving away from simply solving a problem or healing an energy complaint towards more adventurous uses of tapping. Moving away from the negative to the positive is an exciting, relatively new development of EFT. Craig's belief that original EFT was at the bottom of a high rise and his early insistence that we were in uncharted territory and no one knew where EFT was heading, or how far it was capable of progressing, have turned out to be a reality. Yet the benefit of nearly 20 years of worldwide experience has now led tapping into a new arena: positive EFT!

Just as Craig was Callahan's star pupil, a similar story could be told about Dr Silvia Hartmann, who became Craig's gold star protégé and we shall be exploring her work in greater detail in future chapters. Taking the energy modality from simply solving negative problems to a more positive orientation was a fairly natural development for tapping, because enthusiasts like Craig and Hartmann were always looking to extend the borders and see how far they could take this extraordinary methodology.

Naturally inquisitive practitioners like the aforementioned are big personalities within the therapeutic family and the founder's 'hands-free' attitude and approach gave EFT a flexible, broad enough base to facilitate and accommodate unique personalities such as Craig and Hartmann within its framework. These geniuses were able to have the necessary vision to explore more creative possibilities for EFT. Moreover, and this is important, they used EFT a fair proportion of their time on themselves in terms of self-application. This without doubt sped up their own innate healing processes. Freeing themselves from their own energy disturbances certainly helped EFT itself to evolve as they evolved! As we are given the gift of EFT for purposes of evolution, in turn EFT the modality – the 'EFT entity' – is given the gift of its own evolution through its practitioners of EFT. This is a wonderful example of symbiosis: in positive energy exchange everybody and everything within its environment gets to positively benefit, to positively change and to evolve. This is an advanced principle of energy work and EFT: the future of EFT is evolution!

Both Craig and Hartmann are great examples of the kind of plants that have grown and flourished in the new soil of the New Age environment. Craig has always been open about his spiritual beliefs. As a young man he had a profound spiritual experience, which connected him to the source of pure love that is outside time and space and fills the whole universe. This could be viewed as a state of enlightenment.

This realisation that we are all one, and connected to God, is clearly far removed from conventional Western thinking; however, it is reflected to some extent in the beliefs of the New Age movement and Eastern philosophy. Craig is also a student of *A Course in Miracles*, which is a channelled book, supposedly based directly on the words of Jesus himself, with the aim of bringing all people into enlightenment.

The most advanced forms of EFT now aim to tap people into this enlightened condition. If Craig's achievement was to make tapping accessible to the common folk, then Hartmann's contribution to the development of EFT is to introduce a positive side to the treatment. This has been primarily achieved by the replacement of the SUD scale (if you remember, the SUD scale measured the emotional discomfort of the presenting problem with the view to reducing the issue to zero) and the introduction of the more extensive SUE scale (Subjective Units of Experience). The SUE scale ranges from minus ten to plus ten, where minus ten is the worst you could possibly feel – a severe catatonic state – and plus ten is the best you could possibly feel – a state of blissful enlightenment.

Hartmann's SUE scale dramatically aims not only to take the client from a negative position on the scale to zero (which is the aim of traditional EFT), but also to move the client up the positive ladder to ultimately taking them to plus ten on the scale – the position of enlightenment. Hartman is interested in bringing clients onto the positive side of the scale where they can experience higher levels of energy that bring about feelings of joy, elation and love. Hartmann is primarily concerned with energy and, for her, tapping is a technique to free the energy blockages to enable energy flow in the body where these positive emotions can be experienced.

So far we have talked much about EFT and in the following pages it is time to walk the talk! The next chapter guides you through your first practical EFT rounds and gives you the opportunity to experience EFT for yourself. Before we begin, why not give yourselves a hearty, congratulatory pat on the back and treat yourself to a glass of mineral enhanced sparkling water to reenergise your senses, or take a refreshing hot beverage of tea or coffee, so that you will be able to fully engross yourself in the wonders of hands-on EFT!

6

Tapping Into the Power of EFT

DIY EFT for the Beginner

Here are seven fabulous EFT exercises for you to have fun with. Take your time to work through these and don't be too surprised to find yourself quickly achieving some great results along the way and learning a tremendous amount of tapping in a short space of time as you playfully experience practical EFT.

EFT is wonderful for working on all kinds of emotional issues. So, we now invite you to pick a problem. Think for a moment about something that disturbs you or makes you feel uncomfortable. Here are a few examples to help you get the idea: anger, anxiety, worry, fear, stress, obsessive thoughts, lack of confidence, etc. In our first example, we will use stress as the problem emotion. You can substitute the word stress for the particular emotion you are experiencing. We are going to use Craig's modern EFT protocol.

Exercise one: your first self-help EFT treatment session

- First, tune into that emotion. How strongly do you feel that emotion at this moment in time? How stressed do you feel?

- Measure this on the SUD scale (from ten – extreme feelings, to zero – no feelings).

- Now we begin the Set Up: 'Even though I feel stressed, I completely love and accept myself.' We say this out loud three times while tapping the karate chop point. As we tap, we remember to breathe fairly deeply to help the energy flow.

- We now tap on the first point, which is the top of the head, with our index (first) finger.

- On each out breath we say the reminder phrase 'stress' as we tap rhythmically – not too hard and not too softly – about seven to ten times and then move on to the eyebrow point, then: the corner of the eye; under the eye; under the nose; the chin; collarbone; under the arm; and finally the karate chop point.

- Close your eyes and take a few deep breaths. Then allow your eyes to open. That completes your first round of Craig's revised EFT. Well done. How do you feel now?

- Take another measurement on the SUD scale. If all goes well, the intensity of your emotion has either completely gone to zero on the scale or has at least been reduced. If you have moved to zero, congratulations – you have successfully removed the problem in a single round – hurray! If you haven't yet gone down to zero, progress has likely been made and in this case you are on the right track. Why not tap another round and see if you can go further down the SUD scale?

- The second round begins with a revised Set Up: 'Even though I have a little remaining stress, I totally love and accept myself.' (Repeat the steps as in the first round). Now measure your progress. Continue EFT treatment rounds until you have resolved the issue.

- When you have finished your EFT treatment session, it is a good idea to drink a glass of mineral water to help assist the energy flow.

Before going on to the next exercise, take some time to reflect on your EFT experience. It might be a good idea to write your thoughts down in a notebook; certainly, if you are serious about getting fantastic results using EFT, this is advisable so that you can track your progress. Note how well you did, including your successes and anything that was not so good. Keeping a record of your results helps you to really get good at using EFT.

Exercise two: your first EFT treatment session with a partner

EFT works brilliantly as a self-help treatment; it is also equally effective when used with a partner (someone who is experiencing a problem). Here is an example of how to conduct EFT with another person:

- Let's say your practice partner is feeling anxious. First, you ask them what they are anxious about, and they say they are anxious about a meeting they have tomorrow with their boss.

- We get them to measure this emotion on the SUD scale, and they say it is a seven.

- We then get them to make the Set Up sentence using their own words: 'Even though I have this anxious feeling about the meeting tomorrow with my boss, I totally love and accept myself.' We say this out loud along with our partner three times while tapping the karate chop point.

- We then use a reminder phrase: 'tomorrow's meeting'. We both tap on this phrase. (You may be wondering why it is necessary for you to tap along with your friend. Don't worry about that for now, simply go with the flow and this will become clear as you gain a greater appreciation and understanding of the energy concepts expressed throughout this book.)

- As we tap, we remember to breathe fairly deeply to help the energy flow.

- We now tap on the first point, which is the top of the head, with our index finger.

- On each out breath we say the reminder phrase: 'tomorrow's meeting'. We tap rhythmically – not too hard and not too softly – about seven to ten times and then move on to the eyebrow point, then the corner of the eye; under the eye; under the nose; the chin; collarbone; under the arm; and finally the karate chop point.

- When we have conducted this round we both close our eyes and take a few deep breaths. Then we allow our eyes to open. That completes our first round of EFT with a practice partner. We now ask how we both feel after this round.

- We then take another measurement of our partner's emotional intensity on the SUD scale. Ideally, the intensity of our partner's emotion has either completely gone to zero on the scale or has at least been reduced. If they have moved to zero, congratulations – you have successfully removed the problem in a single round – hurray! If they haven't yet gone down to zero, it is likely that progress has been made and in this case you are on the right track. Why not tap another round with your partner and see if they can go further down the SUD scale?

So now it's your turn. With a partner have a go at conducting an EFT treatment round for yourself.

- Get your partner to pick a problem then measure it on the SUD scale.

- Now get them to come up with a Set Up sentence and shorten this to a reminder phrase as you both tap the karate chop point while saying: 'Even though I feel X (Substitute X for your partner's problem), I totally love and accept myself.' Say this out loud along with your partner three times while tapping the karate chop point.

- Then use a shortened reminder phrase, and both tap on this phrase. As you both tap, you should both remember to breathe fairly deeply to help the energy flow.

- You now tap on the first point, which is the top of the head, with our index finger.

- On each out breath you say the reminder phrase, you tap rhythmically – not too hard and not too softly – about seven to ten times and then move on to the eyebrow point, then: the corner of the eye; under the eye; under the nose; the chin; collarbone; under the arm; and finally the karate chop point.

- When you have conducted this round, you should both close your eyes and take a few deep breaths.

Then allow your eyes to open. That completes your practice partner round of EFT.

- You should now ask how you both feel after this round.

- Take another measurement of your partner's emotional intensity on the SUD scale. All being well, the intensity of your partner's emotion has either completely gone to zero on the scale or has at least been reduced. If they have moved to zero, congratulations – you have successfully removed the problem in a single round – hurray! If they haven't yet gone down to zero, progress may yet have been made and in this case you are on the right track. Why not tap another round with your partner and see if you can go further down the SUD scale?

Right, how did you both do? Hopefully you had a pleasant and enjoyable EFT experience. If your partner is in agreement, why not now switch roles? You can be the patient while your partner is the facilitator.

When you have finished, reflect on the two exercises and notice what you have learnt. You may find it beneficial to jot this down in your notebook.

Do you recall asking the question: 'Why is it necessary for you to tap along with your friend?' Can you possibly answer this question for yourself now? Think about that for a moment…

You probably are familiar with the phrase: 'Two heads are better than one.' Tapping in support of another who is in need of help is nurturing and loving. Ultimately, it is a beautiful thing to do for another person, and on many levels both of you will highly benefit from such a loving interaction.

Exercise three: tapping on your partner

There are times when tapping on a person is helpful. The person in question may be too upset and stressed even to carry out simple EFT instructions. Also, the client or patient may be too ill or even in an unconscious state. The person may additionally be physically incapacitated in some way that would prevent them from tapping for themselves.

Part one

Conduct a round or two of EFT on your practice partner. For this example, agree to tap on 'stress free'.

- Hold your partner's hand and send loving energy into their hand and body. Notice how this makes you feel.

- Begin to tap (no need for any Set Up) on your partner's head and both say on each out breath: 'de-stress'.

- Now continue to conduct a full round of EFT, tapping where appropriate on each tapping point of your partner.

- After the round, carry out an SUD scale measurement of both of you.

- Do subsequent EFT rounds until you are both feeling relaxed and chilled.

Part two

Swap over and get your partner to tap on you.

- Get your partner to hold your hand and send loving energy into your hand and body. Notice how this makes you feel.

- Get your partner to begin to tap (no need for any Set Up) on your head and both say on each out breath: 'de-stress'.

- Get your partner to continue to conduct a full round of EFT tapping on each of your EFT points.

- After the completion of the EFT round, carry out a SUD scale measurement of both of you.

- Do subsequent EFT rounds until you are both feeling relaxed and chilled.

Part three

Reflect on these two experiences. Write a short review of what you have both learnt in your EFT notebook.

Exercise four: EFT on the phone

You may be surprised to discover that EFT can be wonderfully successfully conducted on the phone. Here is an opportunity for you to experience this first hand.

Part one

- Phone a practice partner.

- Get them to present you with a problem.

- Explain to them what EFT is and guide them through an EFT treatment round while on the phone. Here is the sequence for you.

  - Explain to them what EFT is and outline the EFT process.

  - Get them to measure their emotion on the SUD scale.

  - Get them to make the Set Up sentence using their own words: 'Even though I have X, I totally love and accept myself.' Say this out loud three times, tapping the karate chop point.

- Use a reminder phrase 'X'. Both tap on this phrase.

- As you tap, remember to breathe fairly deeply to help the energy flow.

- Tap on the first point, which is the top of the head, with your index finger.

- On each out breath say the reminder phrase 'X', tap rhythmically – not too hard and not too softly – about seven to ten times and then move on to the eyebrow point, then: the corner of the eye; under the eye; under the nose; the chin; collarbone; under the arm; and finally the karate chop point.

- When you have conducted this round, both close your eyes and take a few deep breaths. Then allow your eyes to open. That completes your first round of EFT tapping on the phone.

- Ask how they feel after this round.

- Take another measurement on the SUD scale. Ideally, the intensity of your phone partner's emotion has either completely gone to zero on the scale, or has at least been reduced. If they have moved to zero, congratulations – you have successfully removed the problem in a single round – hurray! If progress has been made, then you are on the right track. Why not tap another round with your partner and see if you can go further down the SUD scale?

Part two

Now reverse the roles. Get your practice partner to become the facilitator while you become the patient, and begin another EFT phone session.

Review of phone EFT experience

Answer the following questions for both part one and part two.

How well did you both do?

1. Was this EFT treatment practice easier to do on the phone? Explain your reasons.

2. In what way was EFT on the phone different from face-to-face EFT?

3. What did you both learn from this experience?

4. Did you find it got easier as you progressed through the two sessions?

5. Write down your reflections in your EFT notebook.

Exercise five: Proxy Tapping

Another fascinating feature of EFT is that you don't have to be physically present with the patient to help them and for EFT to be effective. When call tapping on ourselves on behalf of another Proxy Tapping. It is a marvellously useful form of EFT.

Let's imagine that you have a loved one who is ill in hospital. You can now conduct a few EFT rounds to help them to release stress and anxiety and aid the healing process. You can do it any time of day or night with or without their knowledge in the comfort of your home. This is an enormous benefit of EFT!

• Pick a person you would like to Proxy Tap for.

• Tune into that person's energy (use your intuition/imagination).

- Take an SUD reading – imagine how your friend is now feeling (go on – have a go at this; if you get stuck, just pretend and give a measurement).

- Conduct an EFT round in the usual way.

- Assess how you now feel.

- Take another SUD reading.

- Tap subsequent rounds until you feel energised and experience a sense of completeness.

- If appropriate, can you find out how your patient is doing?

Review of Proxy Tapping Exercise

Well done! Isn't that great? Think of how useful Proxy Tapping could be for you, your family, your friends, your work colleagues, your loved ones and your pets!

Exercise six: EFT your cat!

Have you or has your fellow EFT practice partner got a pet? A moggy or a doggy, a fishy or a snaky? Good! We can, believe it or not, EFT (used here as a verb) our animal friends. We can do this in two ways: directly tap on them or Proxy Tap on them. As you can now appreciate, the life of the EFTer is never dull or boring – we have plenty of opportunities to tap on ourselves, our significant others and, of course, even on our pets!

Animals, like humans, have emotional challenges from time to time. We can EFT their problems away and save on the vet's bills! Pets' problems invariably end up being our problems too if we don't take some sort of action, so judicious tapping on our furry friends can be highly fruitful for all concerned. We all love our pets, and now you can show your love by treating them to some much-deserved EFT rounds!

- Pick a pet.

- Either gently tap directly on him or her or Proxy Tap on their behalf.

- Continue additional EFT rounds until you achieve the desired result: a chilled, happy feline or canine.

- Assess your experience and record it in your EFT notebook.

Exercise seven: EFT all your issues away!

Take your wonderful EFT notebook and jot down any problems that you are currently facing right now. (You haven't got any – brilliant! Ask your friend! You haven't got a friend? Perfect – tap on that!) If you are fairly new to EFT, you probably have your fair share of challenges like most of us, so now you have a golden opportunity to begin to tap on them. Just remember – only one at a time please! Take your most pressing challenge and begin an EFT treatment round or take your favourite problem – have fun with this!

This concludes Chapter 6. Why not treat yourself to a much-deserved rest. Put up your feet up with a cup of tea or coffee and simply enjoy a few moments of peace and calm. When you are ready, move on to Chapter 7 where you will read about some real-life EFT stories including an insight into both authors' initial personal experiences of EFT and how this changed their lives for the better. See you soon.

7

Real-life Stories of EFT at Work

We begin Chapter 7 with the authors recounting their initial experiences with EFT.

Emergency EFT to the rescue

Lawrence Pagett's EFT story

I don't recall this as being my first ever self-help EFT session, yet it certainly sticks in my mind as a fond reminder illustrating how downright down to earth practical EFT can be.

Some years back, while at university, I trapped my hand in a window while attempting to close it. This resulted in a badly cut hand. At the time I was alone. There was a fair amount of blood, and I was in pain and suffering from mild shock. Thankfully, I immediately started tapping with my able-bodied hand. At first, nothing seemed to happen, then surprisingly, within no more than a couple of minutes, my emotional fear and confusion curiously started to vanish and the pain had reduced considerably.

After a few more rounds of Craig-style EFT, the emotional discomfort had completely evaporated and there was just a mild throbbing in my hand. The whole experience left me curiously empowered and energised to the point that I actually enjoyed the event. This unforgettable incident was sufficient to convince me of the powerful effectiveness of EFT.

What was amazing to me at the time was how rapidly my thinking had changed from one of blind panic to clarity of focus and thought after just a couple of EFT rounds. Although my mind at first attempted to keep reliving the trauma, the memory no longer felt fearful – the sting of the emotional intensity had gone. Instead, I saw the incident in a non-attached way. I saw it for what it really was – a tiny inconvenient accident of no real consequence. Moreover, I had the insight that with EFT, it is literally at the tip of your finger! Once you know EFT, it stays with you wherever you go. On that particular day it had been a great replacement for the first aid kit and the ambulance, which I no longer had any need for!

Paul Millward's EnergyEFT story

PRACTITIONER'S PERSPECTIVE

I went round to visit Paul one evening; he was about to have his tea when I arrived. I told him about EFT and he was only remotely interested. Energy wise, I would say he was about a plus one or two on the SUE scale. I monitored myself to be at a slightly higher level of, say, plus three.

After he had finished his evening repast, I ventured to introduce EnergyEFT to him and he chivalrously agreed to take part in his first ever round of energy tapping, Hartmann-style. I methodically explained what it was and how to do it, being careful not to 'suggest' to him its outstanding possibilities, as he is a highly suggestible person and I am a hypnotherapist!

We have a natural rapport because of our longstanding friendship and we share many common interests. I must admit that, like Paul, I didn't really expect too much to happen on that night conducting a beginner's guide to a single EFT round.

As soon as Paul started to tap on the top of his head, the atmosphere in the room began to change, and by the time he got to the under the nose/lip position (shaving foam position – the sixth position), he couldn't stop laughing. Energetically, it was a sweet moment, like a child giggling. It then became an extraordinary priceless occasion – one that we could all so easily have missed if I hadn't made the effort to introduce this foreign EFT concept to him and if he had declined to accept to take part.

I'll now let Paul convey this to you in his own way using his own words…

TAPPING INTO THE BLISS

Here is an account of my first experience of EFT. At the time this occurred, I knew nothing about EFT, but the experience was so profound that it led to me becoming fascinated by the EFT process.

What follows is an extract from something I wrote about the experience at the time it happened. In the cold light of day it may sound extravagant and excessive, but it was written as an honest and very candid description of the experience, not originally intended for public consumption.

However, I would like to share it with you now as it is a wonderful example of the miraculous way that EFT can sometimes work – instantly bringing a person to plus ten on the SUE scale – the place of enlightened love and bliss.

It was quite late in the evening when my good friend Lawrence came round, keen to try out an EFT tapping session with me. I had just eaten my tea and was feeling quite tired. At this point I didn't feel particularly optimistic about the possible effects that this 'tapping' process might have. Conditions did not seem conducive for a particularly exciting outcome. It seemed improbable that something so apparently simple could have the dramatic results that

Lawrence had talked about – how could tapping various bits of my face with a finger and repeating a single word change my life?

Lawrence talked about Hartmann's SUE scale: minus ten to plus ten – catatonic hell to ecstatic bliss. I was probably feeling about plus one or two, so rather than focusing on the negative and getting into something too heavy, we decided to tap on something positive to see where it might take me on the scale. Not expecting anything revolutionary to happen I began to tap on the word 'joy', but within minutes I felt some irrepressible glee bubbling up inside. I began giggling like a child as the weight of the world flew away; all worries and problems dissolved.

As the tapping continued I fell into ecstasy – I was dancing with angels, floating in a heavenly realm of light and bliss! It was overwhelming, like being intoxicated with some magical drug as my former mundane self was deflated, flattened and forgotten, and I soared reborn into the skies. I had miraculously been jettisoned to plus ten on the scale within mere moments!

I was shocked and astonished at how this apparently simple procedure, so easy a small child could follow it, could have such instant success and be so transformative. It was incredibly powerful and as I began to recover from this first extraordinary session I was intrigued to see what would happen if we tapped on the word 'girls', a subject close to my heart.

Initially I thought this would just be a bit of fun, but as I tapped and repeated the word 'girls', something truly momentous began to unfold, which took my breath away. I entered a state of sublime ecstasy as a feminine presence of ineffable sweetness completely enveloped me. Images of delectable young women with heavenly limbs floated towards me, their innocent tender love caressing my soul.

My body glowed and tingled in response – this was more real and more palpable than any actual physical contact with a woman could ever be. I had connected with the spiritual essence of Woman and it was the sweetest joy imaginable.

The tapping continued but now I was in free flow, allowing the muse to take me where it would as a whole series of cherished feminine images began to flow through me as I reached higher and higher into bliss: Botticelli's Venus, Waterhouse's Lady of Shalott, the voice of Liz Fraser from the Cocteau Twins and Maria Callas. Then the spirit of female saints seemed to enter my spirit, climbing into the deepest regions of my heart, the purity of their love and joy enrapturing me.

Not bad for a Wednesday night.

Two real-life examples of phone EFT

Mario Jenkins' EnergyEFT story

Practitioner's perspective

Mario has been a friend of mine since way back. One evening I gave him a ring to catch up on things and he said he had been suffering from a backache. I explained about EnergyEFT and he agreed to have a go at it. He was very tired and he was speaking incredibly slowly; energy wise, he was certainly on the negative side of the SUE scale – say a minus three.

This proved to be an extremely ponderous affair. We tapped on the word 'low' (low back pain) and boy was this slow – it must have taken 10 to 15 minutes to conduct our first round.

'L-o-w', 'L-o-w', 'L-o-w' (slow). It has to go down as the slowest rounds of EFT I have ever experienced! (Snail paced would be an accurate description here.)

Despite this, it was a wonderfully enjoyable experience akin to leading a small tottering child along a high mountain ridge. Gently…gently…steady. That's right. That's good! Or helping a blind person across a busy street. Energy work is never dull, and it is always fun if you give the experience your full attention and tune into it!

Here's Mario's account.

Mario's EnergyEFT phone story

On 9 September (2012) I had a social phone call from Lawrence, and I happened to mention that I was suffering from some lower back pain due to stress.

Lawrence offered to do some tapping rounds over the phone. Although I was quite tired, and I thought it would be an effort to concentrate on the instructions, Lawrence's tone was slow and calm. I followed his instructions to tap on the centre of the head, the face and then over the heart area.

I began to notice that the discomfort level in my lower back felt slightly better, and my own energy level was increased. By the second round, as I told Lawrence, I think I had moved from a minus three to maybe a plus five or plus six (on the SUE scale). Something had clearly shifted.

I was definitely more energised by the whole EFT experience. My back pain was not as bad, and within two days of rest and paracetamol, I was back to normal.

Wendy Howard's EnergyEFT story

Practitioner's perspective

I have known Wendy and been aware of her 'problem' for many years. One night she phoned up in a highly disturbed emotional state. She was screaming, sobbing and blurting out incoherent babble in an endless stream. She clearly was in full flood and it was impossible to interrupt this highly emotional pattern of behaviour she was submerged in. So I just listened and hoped she would come up for breath. Eventually my patience was rewarded when she cried out: 'If you are so clever why don't you help me? My emotions are running wild – I can't stop them. I don't know what to do. I'm desperate please help me do something – I need a miracle!'

I explained calmly that I could help her if she was prepared to follow some simple instructions. What happened next is what sets EFT apart from any other intervention, and what makes EFT a potential lifesaver at times. Let's let Wendy take over from here...

Wendy's EFT phone session
My name is Wendy.

As a child, due to my upbringing, I was never able to release emotions. The 'norm' for me was to go off and quietly play with my toys, bottling up the 'hurts' I'd received. The comfort I received was keeping my things tidy and in order. Not surprisingly then, as an adult, when faced with emotional issues, I developed obsessive compulsive disorder (OCD) as a way of coping. Now, if I'm hurt or upset about anything, the OCD will noticeably increase. Although this seems alright on the surface, a problem occurs when the OCD becomes so intense *it* becomes the problem! Then, when *it* breaks, the emotions are left bare. Now, I cannot cope with all the tidying up the OCD demands, and I have never learnt to cope with the emotions that are now coming out 'all over the place'! I'm in trouble with a capital 'T'!

On one such occasion, I ran back upstairs to the safety of my bed. There were loads of tears and I felt totally overwhelmed by feelings that I could not handle now coming to the surface. I picked up the phone and asked to speak to Lawrence, a good friend I have known for many years.

I blurted everything out to him, amongst the tears and anger, hoping he'd say something to help me sort myself out. I was in a hopeless state!

I had never before done what he told me to do! With my index and middle finger together, tap your head, now move down to your face, and tap here, carry on, breathing deeply at the same time. I continued doing this 'tapping' and within a very short time (less than a minute) I had completely calmed down! Lawrence, on asking how I felt, then suggested we do another round of the tapping.

When I put the phone down, I was a very different person to the one who picked it up. I calmly got up off the bed and was able to continue with my afternoon as if nothing had happened I didn't even need the OCD, here, to inform me what I should be doing!

On speaking to Lawrence since that day, he told me the 'tapping' has a name – it is known as EFT. I wanted to share my experience here to help others, who, like myself, have difficulty expressing their emotions and have not heard of this way of helping themselves. You can do it in your own home; it costs nothing and it works!

EFT tips

Here are a few tried and tested principles that you may like to incorporate to help improve the quality and results of your EFT sessions.

- *'Try it on anything!'* Craig, the founder of EFT, made this an EFT maxim. Whatever the problem, why not give EFT a go? It is always worth tapping on anything to see if you can bring about change. EFT is that universal and that flexible. As we are fundamentally dealing with energy, you can in theory at least, just as effectively tap on a traffic jam, the inclement weather, a lost or delayed parcel and your stuck finances, as you can on a more traditional subject such as using EFT to remove an anxiety, worry or fear. This takes us nicely onto our next tip…

- *'Tap and see!'* This is like the previous EFT tip but with a subtle difference, and it happens to be a favourite of one of the authors of this book, borne out ofpersonal experience. Sometimes we may feel a certain resistance or 'laziness' to conducting an EFT round. Additionally, we may feel 'shy' about suggesting to a person they use EFT. Nevertheless, just do it! What have you got to lose? Well, possibly quite a lot if you don't do an EFT session, as the following illustrations prove.

(Before we look at our 'Tap and see' stories, let me affirm that, almost without exception, whenever there has been an expressed doubt about whether to do EFT on a certain challenge or not, invariably the author in question has been deeply thankful when he was able to put reservations aside and make the effort to use EFT. He has usually been delighted, and often surprised and greatly rewarded by the decision to 'Tap and see'.) Here, then, are our own true stories around EFT 'Tap and see'.

First, when I invited my co-author and good friend, Paul, to conduct his initial EFT session, I could so easily have let that opportunity slip. Neither of us were feeling particularly inspired at the time – it was well into the evening and we had both had busy days. Yet, how sad it would have been to have missed this wonderful opportunity.

Second, halfway through penning *Principles of EFT (Emotional Freedom Techniques)*, I invited Paul to join me for an EFT round or two on the subject of our book. We decided to tap on the Set Up: 'Principles of EFT Book'.

As soon as we began our round, the energy in the room changed, and we both experienced a profound shift as we were curiously transported in our minds to a forest glade where a party was in full swing. There was dancing, singing and much merry making as the woods were thronged with happy little folk. It quickly became apparent that we had arrived and the fay (fairy people) began including us in their festivities. At this portentous gathering we mortals and our book were being anointed with generous amounts of fairy dust as the celebrations spanned into the night. The result of this experience was deeply joyful and life affirming, and both of us were positively affected by this strange EFT-inspired happening. It completely transformed what would have been a fairly routine afternoon book-writing session into an incredibly uplifting occasion. Once again, it would have been such a shame and a lost opportunity if we had not decided to 'Tap and see' on a particular subject, in this case, our 'EFT book'. Incidentally, even while typing this, months after that summer afternoon experience, I can still feel the energy of the EFT event and my connection with that 'fairy anointing', and I continue to feel a great affection for the energy exchange brought about by following the 'Tap and see' technique.

To sum up then: We use 'Tap and see' when we are unsure whether to use EFT on a particular topic or at a particular time. When we find ourselves in a dilemma, or wonder whether it's worth doing EFT then we simply begin an EFT tapping round and see what, if anything, happens. Be prepared to be amazed!

- *Keep oxygenated*: Fresh air helps EFT sessions and it's free!

- *Keep hydrated*: Good-quality water also aids the EFT process.

- *Remember to move*: Hartmann insists that we stand up and move our bodies to facilitate EFT.

- *Keep an 'EFT pot'*: Here is a super tip for you. Take a container about the size of a small jam jar. It could be a wooden box or anything that you can place small pieces of card or paper in. A used hand-cream pot with a lid will suffice. Now, whenever you have a challenge or a problem, make a note of it, date it and put it into your 'EFT to do later pot', then when you have a free moment, open your pot and take out a challenge and begin to EFT it away! This is especially useful for those stubborn problems. Once you get the hang of conducting EFT regularly, you will be fascinated at how useful an EFT pot becomes. Don't be too surprised to find that after a while you may even run out of things to tap on because you have successfully removed them all by using EFT!

- *De-stress regularly throughout the session*: Make it a goal to remain as stress-free as possible, particularly when conducting EFT. It is a good idea to take regular relaxation breaks to keep you fresh and free from stress. Of course, you can use EFT to do this; however, it is sometimes useful to have a five to ten minute rest away from your EFT session, as this often will not just to improve future rounds of EFT, but also to alleviate the current EFT problem you are working on.

- *Tap all the way to completion*: This is not always practical, but it is always preferable. Hartmann suggests conducting another round of EFT and trying not to stop before you have completely removed the problem.

- *It's only energy*: Write down this phrase 50 times and keep it on your fridge door.

- *Keep focused*: It is essential to stay on track throughout your EFT session. It may be helpful to jot down a few notes in your notebook after each EFT round to keep focused on how well you are progressing. This is especially important when dealing with a complex problem that may have many parts (Craig's 'aspects') to it.

- *Attempt only one problem issue at a time*: Sometimes it is tempting to change direction or to move on to another issue that may come to mind as you are tapping. Again, this is where jotting down how your EFT is going is useful. Often related and unrelated thoughts, images, ideas and 'Aha!' moments may appear to interrupt the flow of the session. Simply note these down so that you can use them for a later time. It is always a good idea to be totally focused on the presenting problem and not get side-tracked by tapping on other unrelated issues that show up. The 'rule' is: 'If it's directly relevant to the problem you are tapping on then fine. If it is not related then note it down and save it for a later EFT session.'

8

What is EnergyEFT?
The Work of Dr
Silvia Hartmann

Congratulations if you are still with us at this point, for right now you have arrived at a significant place within our personal EFT journey. This is particularly true if you have been brave and devoted enough to follow us each and every step of the way. We started our ascent with Chapter 1's introduction to ancient Chinese energy concepts, which explored the deeper history of the origins of EFT and we have continued thus far. So why not give yourself a proverbial pat on the back and shake the dust from off your feet by taking a moment or two of much-deserved rest; simply sit back and reflect on how far you have already come. We invite you to stop for a moment along the roadside to contemplate the wonderful vistas that have opened up before us as the trip has unfolded – perhaps you could notice that you have already learned a substantial amount of EFT and travelled a considerable way along the EFT highway following its many twists and turns and experiencing the joys of the tapping adventure.

Along the way we have met and started to appreciate the significance of ancient shamanic energy principles and practices, complex acupuncture concepts, meridians, New Age scientists, the precursors to EFT and, of course, the founding father of EFT, Craig. Moreover you have had the opportunity to practise and experience for yourselves an array of tapping protocols and techniques to introduce you to the wonders of EFT, and you have started to recognise – theoretically and practically – just how useful tapping can be for you and your family, friends and loved ones.

Take a while to survey the panoramic views that we have already experienced; take a few deep breaths in and right out now, as you allow yourself to consolidate all the learning that this EFT encounter has taught you thus far and simply relax, drift and dream as this integration takes place at the deepest levels of body and mind automatically...

When you are ready to continue along our path together, have a stretch and a glass of water so that you feel fully refreshed and ready to begin the next stage in our EFT exploration.

As fantastic as all the sights, sounds and experiences have been so far, we are now about ready to leave that old habitation way behind as we enter a new world: the world of Dr Silvia Hartmann. It is an enchanting environment that shares some features and familiar landmarks from the original EFT and the tapping that precedes it; however it is certainly a departure from that familiar terrain, and Hartmann's EFT takes us into novel territory in a number of ways. So let's begin to explore the magical realms of Hartmann so that we can uncover what treasure lies before us!

This chapter serves as an appetiser, as an energetic hors d'oeuvre to the rich desserts that await you further along your EFT adventure. It is way beyond the scope of our *Principles of EFT (Emotional Freedom Techniques)* book to include the entirety of Hartmann's extensive body of work. Nevertheless, we do explore some advanced energy concepts here and there are plenty of fascinating ideas and practices for you to absorb and integrate into your EFT experience.

The first thing to realise about Hartmann's EFT is that it concentrates solely on energy. According to Energists like

Hartmann, we have an Energy Body. This may come as a surprise to you because it is a fairly new and curious concept for mainstream Western appreciation. It forms part of the mind-body-spirit relationship, and it is considered to be 'the third field'. In Western thinking we have psychology and physiology and EFT came out of an atmosphere of avant-garde medical Western philosophy that had in turn been influenced by ancient Chinese medical ideas such as acupuncture. It could be argued that this third field, experientially at least, was known by shamans of old and their disciples. This fact is not always immediately obvious, because many of the shamanic techniques were then and are today practised covertly and deliberately kept secret from common folk. What EFT did, among other things, was to make popular energy work and this freely accessible tool required absolutely no knowledge of ancient and traditional energy concepts – this clearly aided its accessibility.

As we have already seen, the 1960s and the New Age movement helped to introduce spiritual practices such as shamanism to a wider Western audience. Do you recall Carlos Castaneda in Chapter 2? He wrote about his experiences with the legendary Mexican sorcerer called Don Juan.

Don Juan introduces his apprentice to how a shaman (sorcerer) tends to see and use energy. Freeing up substantial amounts of energy and learning the art of energy conservation are essential skills for the shamanic practitioner. Often these energy practices enable the participant to see life forms from a purely energetic perspective. Don Juan's magical practices helped him and his followers to experience people as a luminous egg.

Equally fascinating is that Don Juan would occasionally give his subject (in this case Castaneda himself) a surprise sharp bodily slap – an extreme tap if you like – that had the effect of jolting Castaneda out of his normal ordinary

Western thinking into an altered state of consciousness (ASC), placing him into a realm known by his tutor as 'the second attention'.

Hartmann expresses a similar love for energy. She introduces energy and the Energy Body into EFT not as a sideline concept, but as the fundamental tour de force behind her energetic interventions. Hartman's EFT focuses entirely on the third field – the Energy Body. However, she stresses that this fact does not negate the other two fields: the physical body and psychological body. Energists leave the physical body and the psychological body to the doctors and the psychologists. Therefore, if a patient has a physical problem or a mental disease, Hartmann insists that if such problems have not resulted from energy disturbances then they are not of concern to the Energist and are considered to be beyond the bounds of the EFT practitioner. Energists concentrate purely on dealing with the Energy Body. It is the energy disturbances within it that they are attempting to deal with.

Energists are here to help educate their clients and deal with the root of distress and disease found and experienced within the energy system. Hartmann argues that much of the confusion that results from healing interventions of all shapes and sizes comes about largely because this third field has had no place within medical understanding. For the purposes of this book, and to use EFT effectively, it is not necessary to have an in-depth understanding of the Energy Body to practise successful EnergyEFT. In fact, relatively little is known about the Energy Body anyway – it is mysterious and each person's Energy Body is unique to them. The important matter is that we all have an Energy Body and we all have an Energy Mind and these are independent from the physical and psychological parts of us. It is perhaps worth stating here that we are still basically using tapping to help a person remove a problem or assist someone to feel better. In this sense, nothing has changed – we are still using our fingers to tap on EFT points to bring about positive changes. The difference is that we are thinking of these disturbances not so much as emotional issues (though they are emotional, of course), but more accurately as being energy blockages within the Energy Body. We tap on the Energy Body (not the physical body) to remove energy blockages and to allow the stuck energy to flow freely. When we assist the energy flow we help to make the person feel better. Another valid statement of Hartmann's is that often people think that the energy that we are referring to is 'subtle energy'. To Hartmann's mind there is absolutely nothing subtle about it. Energy is powerful! It is obvious! We repeat here: there is nothing subtle about it!

What now follows is a succinct overview of Hartmann's EnergyEFT methodology. We begin with a detailed description of Hartmann's SUE scale and then introduce a number of her EFT protocols.

Hartmann's SUE scale

Just to jog your memory, when EFT was first designed by Craig, he adapted Callahan's TFT measurement scale known as the SUD scale (Subjective Units of Discomfort) and it was used to measure the amount of emotional disturbance that a person felt.

This scale ranged from minus ten to zero, ideal for measuring negative emotions; nevertheless, as we shall soon see, it was limiting and unambitious when dealing with energy and the higher emotional states a person experiences when they are functioning at optimal energetic levels of being. It was for this reason that Hartmann extended the SUD scale to incorporate the full range of positive human emotions with a view to not only removing a client's presenting problem and bringing them to zero, but also to encourage them to achieve even higher states of positive emotion in closer keeping with their true potential. In a nutshell, this is what differentiates traditional EFT from Hartmann's EnergyEFT: exploring and reaching these higher elevated states of consciousness. It's what puts the energy into EFT!

SUE stands for Subjective Units of Experience and the scale ranges from minus ten to plus ten, where minus ten represents the very worst a person could possibly feel, and plus ten represents the very best. (It is important to stress that minus ten is, thankfully, beyond most people's experience and would only include extreme mental conditions such as catatonic schizophrenia, while plus ten is a blissful state of supreme health, joy and enlightenment, which is attainable for all). Zero is the point where the energetic disturbance has been dispersed: the point where energy can begin to flow positively.

For the person who has a problem, reaching zero is a great relief in itself and was in all likelihood the reason why they were tapping in the first place. Take, for example, the person who has a stress headache and conducts one or two rounds of tapping. If the headache is removed by this and no other positive changes are identified, or experienced, then the person could be said to have reached point zero.

EXAMPLE OF THE SUE SCALE

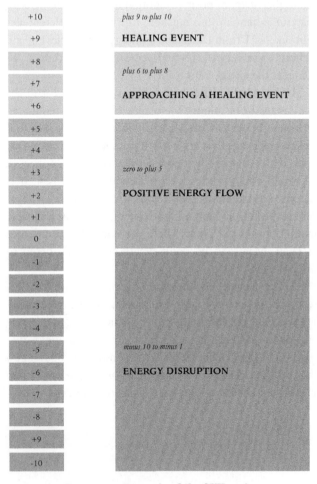

Figure 8.1 Example of the SUE scale

The SUE scale in practice

When applying the SUE scale to an EnergyEFT session, the first step before tapping commences is to ask the client to choose a number on the scale that corresponds to how they currently feel about the emotional issue in order to establish exactly how severe the problem is. Some guidance is needed from the practitioner here to explain the scale to the client, otherwise the client may be applying wildly inaccurate readings that do not correspond to the EnergyEFT practitioner's more realistic understanding of the SUE scale. After each round of tapping the client can be asked to state where they now feel they are on the SUE scale so that you can quantify how the emotional issue is evolving and provide feedback on how the session is progressing. Careful use of the SUE scale provides additional feedback to the participants, giving a subjective guide to how the issue is evolving towards a Healing Event.

Applying the SUE scale brings a rigour to EFT, which helps to not only completely remove the emotional disturbance, i.e. bring the client to point zero, but also to begin to explore the positive side of the SUE scale and make the client feel wonderful rather than simply resolving an issue. In other words, Hartmann is never satisfied with simply removing a problem, she always encourages further rounds of EnergyEFT to take the client to those elevated reaches of energy utilisation that naturally occur when a person experiences the higher realms of plus eight, plus nine and plus ten on the SUE scale.

The Heart and Soul Protocol

The Heart and Soul Protocol is Hartmann's take on conducting an EFT round. According to Hartmann, the heart is like a nuclear reactor – it is the powerhouse of the energy system.

Energy is processed in the heart centre and it manifests itself from that place. In certain spiritual traditions the heart is the spiritual centre of the human being. This is not so alien to the West. We all know that there is a difference between what our heart tells us and what our head tells us. Western science has tended to glorify the head and to a large extent our society is based around head knowledge rather than the more spiritual heart knowledge. The cult of the brain with its concentration on rationality, materialism and analytical thinking stultifies the emotional spiritual truth of who we truly are and insists that we remain focused on the five senses of touch, taste, sight, sound and smell. This preoccupation with material existence is an incredibly narrow form of focus and basically states that if you can't see it, touch it, taste it or smell it, it does not exist – a somewhat naive way of viewing and experiencing reality. While the five senses are useful and the brain and thinking have their place, they should always be subservient to the intelligence of spirit, and it must be acknowledged that there is far more out there than meets the eye!

Healing hands

As well as the significance of the heart, we also acknowledge our hands' ability to heal. This again takes us nicely back to Chapter 1 where primitive man is seen to utilise healing touch to bring love into the equation – always a good thing. Hartmann's Heart and Soul Protocol introduces the concept of 'healing hands' and this elevates EFT from Callahan's and Craig's rather mechanical tapping process towards a more magical/spiritual awareness. It takes it to another level towards a greater emphasis on love.

The index finger is described as being like the shaman's magic wand. In many cultures it is rude to point this finger at another person for this very reason. This fingertip is where most energy is said to come from and therefore it makes perfect sense to use it for our EFT sessions. In Hartmann's EnergyEFT exercise 'Activating the healing hands', we potentiate the fingers by placing them in the heart centre and then we shoot energy through these fingers to the body parts we tap on.

The activating of our healing hands underlines the actuality that we are not tapping on a physical body and we are not tapping with physical hands or physical fingers – we are tapping with our energy hands and using our energy fingers to tap on the Energy Body, which is an energetic entity in and of itself. This energy entity is the third field that Energists concentrate on. This is a profound methodology that perhaps fits more comfortably within a shamanic framework. We are not a physical body – we are pure energy vibrating at a frequency that takes on physical form.

The Heart and Soul Protocol in action

To start our round of EnergyEFT, we begin in the heart healing position by placing our hands on the centre of the chest. This is the position we always start from and finish with. In the Heart and Soul Protocol there are 14 tapping points (see Figure 8.2 below) beginning on the top of the head and conveniently follow the body downwards as follows:

1. Top of the head.

2. Forehead (third eye point).

3. Eyebrow.

4. Side of eye.

5. Under the eye.

6. Above the lip (affectionately called the shaving foam position).

7. Under the lip/the chin position.

8. Collarbone.

9. A walk around the hand starting with the thumb.

10. First/index finger.

11. Second finger.

12. Ring finger ('God gave us five fingers').

13. Little finger/pinkie.

14. End with the karate chop position.

(Readers who have paid attention so far will notice the omission of the under the arm position, and the addition of the third eye point and the use of the ring finger.)

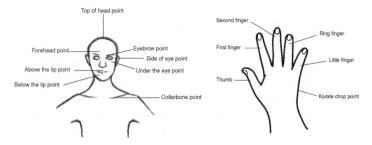

Figure 8.2 The Heart and Soul Protocol tapping points

To begin the session, before starting to tap we further activate our 'healing hands' by shaking them, clapping them, blowing on them and briskly rubbing them together. This helps create our intention and focuses our attention on the task. This should be done in a loving playful manner with a pleasant smile on our faces to evoke a spirit of warmth and gentleness.

Next we turn our attention to the Set Up by placing our hands in the healing heart position. We now take three deep breaths and make the first Set Up statement out loud.

The Set Up statement is a sentence in the present tense that describes the issue or problem in its most general immediate terms. For example, a person who is angry with their boss may use a Set Up sentence like: 'I am angry with my boss.' This statement should communicate the full emotional feeling behind the problem – the person may choose and be encouraged to use a more vernacular vocabulary like: 'I am pissed off with my f***ing boss!!!' The more honest and direct the statement is, the more effective the Set Up becomes. Additionally, if the person shouts this or even screams it, giving vent to their angry emotion, this would be considered a more positive expression of the problem and would be encouraged.

At this juncture it may be worth noting that EnergyEFT is effective at dealing with extreme emotional disturbances such as post-traumatic stress disorder (PTSD) and it would be advisable, in this case, to seek the guidance of a professional EFT practitioner.

Now we theoretically begin to tap our first round of EnergyEFT. We can use either hand and, as the body is symmetrical, we can tap on either side of the head and body. To maintain concentration while conducting a Hartmann round of EFT, a reminder phrase is repeated. This is usually a shorter version of the Set Up sentence – a key word or two that sums up the Set Up phrase. In our example of 'I am angry with my boss', we could use the reminder phrase 'angry' or 'boss'. Using the index finger, begin to tap lightly on the top of the head in a steady rhythmic way. Tap each energy point about seven to ten times and with each exhalation of breath the reminder phrase is spoken or sung out loud.

At the completion of the round the person returns to the healing heart position and takes three deep breaths. An assessment is now made to see what has changed. EFT can have such a powerful, immediate effect on a person that a single round, or even less, can completely deal with the presenting issue. This is extraordinary and is what sets energy work apart from traditional psychological therapeutic modalities.

If the problem has not completely gone away, in all likelihood something will have changed. The angry employee after the initial round may comment that they are no longer furious but are disappointed with their boss's behaviour. The angry emotion has been reduced quite substantially. Therefore the next round of EFT may contain the Set Up: 'I am disappointed with my boss', with the reminder phrase being 'disappointed'. After this round the client has a smile on her face and says: 'My boss can be a bit annoying at times and I was rather snappy first thing this morning.' After some reflection she adds: 'I guess she is only doing her job', and the emotional intensity is further reduced. Additional rounds of EFT may be necessary to eradicate this issue and leave the client in a positive energy state.

The significance of Energy Body stress

We are constantly being assaulted by all manner of stress. We encounter stress from the immediate environment in the form of electromagnetic fields of energy, chemicals, pesticides, toxins, poisons and additives found within our food and water supplies and consumer products such as toothpaste, hairspray, etc. Additionally, we experience mental stress and, finally and relevant to this book, we have Energy Body stress.

Stress accumulates, and once it reaches a critical mass, it adversely affects us in a variety of ways: people can't sleep and when they do sleep the natural healing processes found within healthy sleep break down and eventually a person can become seriously ill with nervous breakdown. Hardcore physical sickness such as heart attacks, strokes and degenerative diseases like Parkinson's could be caused in part by severe stress.

Once we get to illnesses such as those mentioned above, these, of course, need to be treated by a doctor. However, such illnesses often do have an emotional component to them and if they have been caused by stress, EFT can be an invaluable tool to help at the very least to aid the patient to feel emotionally more comfortable around such enormous life challenges.

Stress talk

When a person is under a lot of stress, one of the principle symptoms is what Hartmann calls 'stress talk'. When we are highly stressed we tend to talk gobbledegook in the form of a constant stream of incoherent babble. A person may say all kinds of scary things such as: 'I am mad', 'I want to kill myself' and other grossly exaggerated comments.

We need not be worried or overconcerned about this behaviour, as this is just 'stress talk'. The person is over-stressed and usually doesn't mean or believe what they are saying. When we remove Energy Body stress from a client's energy system, as a consequence they always talk more sensibly and behave more rationally – this is structural. Remove the stress and you bring peace, harmony and mental stability back into the picture and the client begins to make more sense. *Always. There is no exception to this!*

In the past, EFTers would create Set Ups from the garbled stream of words presented to them by extremely upset clients rather than appreciating that these emotional outbursts were a symptom of stress talk. Generally speaking, this approach often had little impact on the real issue behind the stress talk and only served to remove a little of the stress around the underlying issue. Back in the day, countless rounds of EFT would result in very little headway being made. An example may help to explain this. A person says:

> I hate myself, I want to end my life, I want to shoot my cat and set fire to my neighbour's garage because a spaceship is docked in it. They have been communicating with aliens and they have tried to get me abducted. I told the police and they hate me too and want to put me in a mental asylum.

A person presenting problems like this in the past, before we knew about stress talk, would have been a nightmare for the EFT therapist. Where do you begin? 'Even though I hate myself…I totally love and accept myself…'

To make matters worse, this person is rolling around on the floor screaming and making life very difficult for the therapist. In fact, the client is almost impossible to tap on! Moreover, the therapist is now freaking out along with the client and wishing they had never gone on that EFT course or put an EFT ad in the local paper.

Okay, as a layperson reading this book, thankfully you probably will never have to deal with such extreme cases; however, when a relative phones you in floods of tears shouting and swearing because they say their husband has left them, this is not such an untypical emotional response. We have all had to deal with a very upset Aunty Sally or Uncle Jim or an excessively angry boss or work colleague. Such outbursts may not be everyday experiences for most of us, however.

Once we realise that all this abnormal behaviour is just stress talk then it becomes relatively easy to deal with. We simply tap on 'Stress', not on the aliens, the murderous thoughts, the fear of mental illness, the police or the cat you were about to shoot.

We tap to remove Energy Body stress. Remove the stress and after a few rounds we have a much more stable client (and therapist) who has calmed down considerably and both of you are now able to view the challenges from a much more sensible, coherent perspective. Suddenly the client is sounding more rational and intelligent and they are able to admit that they didn't really mean the majority of what they said. Once the stress is gone we can then get the client to tell us what the real problem is and make suitable Set Ups from that vantage point.

Stress talk and stress in general are endemic in our society and worthy of being taken seriously in the context of everyday life and mental illness. One other point that may be helpful for an EFT beginner is to remember that stress is contagious. When a person is acting out of a place of extreme stress this can easily be like a fire, and begin to burn everything in its path. One needs to be mindful of this when doing energy work. We need to put the fire out – not be consumed by it! This is easier to achieve when we recognise that all this exaggerated behaviour is only stress talk – it's only Energy – and from this position we can effectively redirect it and tap it away.

It can be enormously reassuring to realise that when faced with a person who is severely stressed and is saying all kinds of strange and terrible things that everything they are saying is simply not real. It is meaningless nonsense resulting from a highly stressed individual. This realisation allows us to be objective about their situation and rather than allowing ourselves to be seduced into believing the nonsense they are spouting (and by so doing becoming stressed ourselves), this knowledge enables us to remain calm, stress free and in complete control of the EFT session.

How to deal with stress talk

When we are faced with a highly stressed individual, the first thing we need to do is to tap together on removing stress. The Set Up sentence could be simply 'Stress' or 'De-stress', and the reminder phrase would be the same. After an initial round we would test the client's response on the SUE scale and continue following EFT rounds until the stress has been reduced to zero or higher on the SUE scale.

If a person is very stressed, sometimes tapping on physical parts of the body may actually produce even more stress or at least fail to remove it. In this case, a technique known as Proxy Tapping can be effective. Proxy Tapping is when we tap on ourselves on behalf of the client or we may choose to tap on the client ourselves – this can also be very powerful, particularly when an individual's Energy Body and Energy Mind are highly disturbed.

Once we have dealt with the client's stress, we can do an additional round or two tapping on 'Energy' to take both practitioner and client towards the positive side of the SUE scale. Once this has been achieved, we are able to move on to the client's particular issue. It is important to mention that stress is not a once-only experience. Throughout the session, both client and practitioner can have a build-up of stress, and it's useful to be aware of this fact. When we become more confident with our use of the SUE scale, it is a good idea to measure our own stress levels to make sure that we too remain as stress free as possible and take suitable action when we do get stressed.

Hartmann's EFT is concerned with energy, and it's good to remember that the Energy Body extends way outside of the physical body, therefore this energy may interact with everybody and everything it comes in contact with. A client's Energy Body may well intermingle with your Energy Body and vice versa – suddenly we could conceivably have a single energy interconnection. It is useful to know this as it has negative as well as positive implications!

Hartmann stresses that all energy work should be non-hierarchical and that the helper and the helped should work together in order to bring about positive energetic change. EnergyEFT is an equal partnership where a co-operative, interconnected energetic relationship exists. This is a fundamental departure from the 'heartless' doctor–patient relationship, which traditionally has been a rather formal, reserved experience that tends to last a relatively short length of time. In EnergyEFT we work alongside the client as a team. We aid the healing process by tapping on ourselves on behalf of the client. In this way we have two energy entities working together to form a third energetic entity known as 'the EFT team'. We shall explore the wonders of Energy entities in more detail later in our Hartmann EnergyEFT exploration.

The EFT Story Protocol

When a person has a problem, it is important to bear in mind that this issue has a history. Doctors call this a case history, whereas in EFT we call this the EFT Story. Most, if not all, problems have a story to them: a start (when the problem first began), a middle and an end. This may not, however, always be apparent to the person with the problem. According to EFT thinking, when a person has a specific problem then there is always a specific blockage in the energy system. By getting the client to tell their story we are then able to map out the precise details and moments when these blockages first took place. In every story there will be a possible number of blockages, some more severe than others. By getting the client to tell their story we can write it down and pay attention to exactly where these disturbances are in terms of time and space.

These moments when a disturbance takes place are known by Hartmann as 'Energy System Events'. To conduct excellent EFT we need to find these events and tap on them sequentially, one at a time, to bring about what EFT calls a Healing Event (when a client's problem is completely healed). Hartmann states that when dealing with severe stories such as rape and post-traumatic stress disorder we are advised to go gently and tap on the least disturbing events first. Moreover, it is helpful to make sure the client and practitioner remain as stress free as possible throughout the EFT Story Protocol.

Recently, one of the authors had a client who came for their first session and presented a long list of problems that she wanted help with: anger, jealousy, fear, worry, low self-esteem, paranoia, confidence and violent tendencies.

These are very general issues and it would have been ill advised to attempt to tap on all of them in one session, so after the client had been de-stressed she was asked, which out of all the problems would she like to deal with first, and she said 'self-esteem'. So the next question to her was: 'When did all this lack of self-worth begin?' She then started to tell her story. If she had not been de-stressed beforehand, it is likely that she would not have been able to tell what Hartmann describes as 'a well-formed story': one that is coherent, sequential and linear.

This client, once she had been de-stressed and empowered by an additional round or two of EFT to energise her, found it remarkably easy to remember that her lack of confidence and low self-esteem had begun at a specific moment in her past when she had been three years old and her father had ridiculed her in front of the rest of the family. She then went on to tell her 'well-formed story' in a way that was clear and easy to understand, and it was obvious to both client and practitioner where and what events needed to be tapped on and in what particular order. Before she had come for her appointment she had had only a vague recollection of where that self-esteem issue had come from. Additionally, after the initial de-stressing and energising rounds of EFT, she felt that if she dealt with this particular problem by using the EFT Story Protocol, then much of her list of problems she had presented at the start of the session would be easier to handle in later sessions.

The EFT Story Protocol is a very effective method of dealing with the various components that make up a complex or particularly extreme emotionally disturbed problem. By laying out the issue in a series of steps it becomes easier for both patient and practitioner to deal with each part that makes up the whole of the problem.

In the above example it would be possible to tap on each general issue – anger, jealousy, fear, worry, paranoia, low self-esteem, confidence and violent tendencies – one at a time by simply improving the energy flow throughout the treatment and get impressive results. That is precisely what makes EFT great! However, the EFT Story Protocol is beneficial and really shines when dealing with complex issues that cannot be solved through a more general tapping approach.

The Energy Mind

We have already been introduced to the idea that we have an Energy Body, which is in addition to the physical body. We now briefly turn our attention to the Energy Mind, which is also extra to the physical brain/psychological mind. If the heart is the powerhouse of the energy system then the Energy Mind is the computer software that decodes energy units into a language we can appreciate and understand. In traditional psychology, we have the unconscious or subconscious. In Hartmann's EnergyEFT this is called the Energy Mind.

Interestingly, we experience many problems through dysfunctional thinking. We equate our problems with psychological issues: they are 'all in the mind'. In Hartmann's EFT, these mental problems are structurally caused by energy disturbances and low frequencies on the negative side of the SUE scale. When we unblock energy disturbances and move along the SUE scale, flowing our energy in a positive direction, our thinking becomes more rational, coherent and intelligible. Our mental state is a reflection of where we are on the SUE scale at any given moment in time. When energy is positively flowing and evolving then we think sensible, loving and rational thoughts as well as feeling emotionally stable. They go hand in hand: positive energy flow equals sanity and peace of mind. In this sense, negative thinking and abnormal behaviour are not the problem, they are symptoms of the problem: blocked energy. Flow the energy and the negative thinking and abnormal behaviour resolve themselves – they simply vanish. To Hartmann, this is structural and always holds true – there are no exceptions. This is a profound realisation: when we are at plus eight or above on the SUE scale we really have no problems!

The EFT Body Protocol

The EFT Body Protocol is a great way of directly dealing with a person's problems. We simply ask the client to show us with their hands where the energy disturbance is located: 'Where do you feel that feeling [problem] in your body?' In this protocol there is little need for long-winded verbal explanations – no story telling, we simply get to the nitty-gritty. What indeed could be simpler? We then tap to move this stuck feeling (energy) and get the energy to flow out of the energy system. When we successfully do that, we solve the problem!

Ways to use the EFT Body Protocol

The EFT Body Protocol has 101 uses. For example, you can use it effectively on:

- a person who is extremely depressed and verbally uncommunicative

- a business man or woman who has a dark secret (secret therapy) or who is unwilling to divulge their issue

- a dim-witted bloke

- a person who clearly identifies with their physical discomfort

- a person in extreme shock

- and, of course, on practically anybody with an energy-related problem.

A PRACTICAL EXAMPLE

Jeremy comes to see you and he is extremely upset. He says his whole world is falling apart. He then catalogues a series of problems – losing his job; loss of confidence; impending divorce and death of a loved one – all in the space of one month.

'Alright Jeremy, how are you now feeling?'

'Terrible. My legs are wobbly, my head feels like it has a tight metal band strapped around it and I feel like there's a hunk of concrete stuck in my stomach. It also seems like a black cloud is hanging over me!'

We now have a number of physical descriptions that we can tap on. We ask Jeremy to pick one. He chooses the hunk of concrete in his stomach. So we get him to stand up and place one of his hands on this feeling and invite him to rub his stomach gently while we both tap an EFT round together on 'this hunk of concrete'.

After the first round it has moved into his throat. We then conduct another round of EFT and the disturbed energy has noticeably moved again in an upwards direction. It has got smaller and lighter and is now only the size of a golf ball in his head. He feels much better and as a result there is a smile on his face. Energy is clearly moving and this is reflected in his tummy, which is rumbling. Another EFT round and the ball has vanished. Jeremy is delighted and is jumping up and down for joy! We now ask him to comment on how his legs feel and he says they feel fine. Further questioning reveals that he no longer has a black cloud or a metal band around his head.

Aspects

Those of us who are familiar with Craig's EFT will have already come across the term 'aspects'. His understanding of this term relates to parts that make up a problem. For example, a person who has a fear of spiders may say that there are a number of things that they don't like about spiders: the hairy body, scary eyes, the speed they move at and the colour – these are points that we can tap on as they make up and contribute to the overall phobia. Craig calls these 'aspects' of the problem. When we tap only on 'spiders', without a further examination into the component parts that make up the fear or energy disturbance, then we may well deal with this fear relatively quickly in a single round or two. This of course is always preferable; however, it is not always possible and in extreme emotional disturbances it may even be ill advised to do so. The decision of whether to globally tap on an issue or break it down into component parts and tap on each part of the issue is going to depend on a number of variables and this is where the expertise of the practitioner may become of paramount importance.

In Hartmann's terminology 'aspects' has a completely different meaning – it has nothing to do with component parts that make up a problem.

In the world of Hartmann, an 'aspect' is a snapshot of a particular energetic entity in a split second moment in time and space. We all go through time and space, and the world splits these moments into segments of time that scientists measure with clocks. Energists are primarily concerned with the Energy Body and Energy Mind, and describe the world in terms of energy. We could say that an 'aspect' is a person at any given point in time and Hartmann makes it clear that a person can only truly say 'I' in the precise present moment of existence – a nanosecond before or a nanosecond after is no longer you, it is an 'aspect' of a you, not the actual person!

An example here will make this more real and understandable. Here is my recounting of a story in the traditional way:

> When I was four years old I went to school for the first time with my 26-year-old mother. I remember wearing grey shorts and a little red cap. I had knobbly knees. My mum was very young and beautiful and I was very unhappy at the prospect of ten years' imprisonment, which adults laughably called school and the best years of their lives. It was many, many, many years ago!

According to Hartmann, it is untenable to talk about past moments in this manner because those past memories are not who we are now. Therefore using 'I' is not appropriate when talking about past situations. At the moment of writing this, one of the authors is 53 and his mum is 77. We don't look the same as we did; we are, in fact, completely different beings from those halcyon 1960s days. Therefore it is much more helpful and truthful to say it in this way.

> When an *aspect* of me was four years old he went to school for the first time with his 26-year-old *aspect* mother. I remember my *aspect* wearing grey shorts and a little red cap. He had knobbly knees. His *aspect* mum was very young and beautiful and he was very unhappy at the prospect of ten years' imprisonment, which adults laughably called school and the best years of their lives. It was many, many, many years ago!

This is equally true when we talk about anything in the past or the future. It matters not how far in the past or how far in the future. Yesterday is the territory of *aspects* and so is tomorrow. The only place where this doesn't hold good is the place of *now*.

Incidentally, the concept of aspects may have been recognised by other spiritual traditions, for it is obliquely mentioned in the Bible by St Paul. In one of his more mystical reflective moods we read in the New Testament that the apostle, when writing to Corinth describes a past aspect of himself in this way:

> I know a man in Christ who 14 years ago was caught up to the third heaven. Whether it was in the body or out of the body I do not know – God knows. And I know that this man – whether in the body or apart from the body I do not know, but God knows – was caught up to paradise. He heard inexpressible things, things that man is not permitted to tell. (2 Corinthians: 12:2)

This raises another point of interest: esoteric and spiritual experiences are difficult for the 'egoic' self to accept. By shifting our awareness from the physical 'I' to an energy aspect it makes it much easier for us to operate in these other realms and worlds. It makes them more tangible, believable and real.

'As incredible as all this sounds, what has this got to do with EFT and why is all this important?' you may be asking your aspect selves.

First, aspects are important because they help illuminate the shaman's way. This is helpful, arguably, because at least it offers Western rational minds a framework in which to place energy work. Without such a context, many would find EnergyEFT inaccessible and possibly not even credible. Also, this is a fairly advanced energy concept that does take some getting used to. Despite this, if you are serious about advancing your EFT skills then we strongly urge you to hold on in there with us as we further explore this fascinating subject in a little more detail.

Second, the aspect model has many positive practical uses. For one thing, it allows us to deal with our aspect's (and other folks' aspects) past problems in a new and exciting way. We have a tendency to see past experiences as having taken place at a fixed moment in time: something has physically happened to someone that has affected them emotionally, which cannot possibly be undone. The concept of aspects allows us to go into these past experiences to interact with them and, by using EFT, change them; in this way we can use EFT to undo the things that have perhaps bound us up in pain and misery for many years and be freed from them. Now we have a tool and a methodology to literally change the past! That is really amazing when you stop to think about it for a minute or two...

Third, we are not limited to changing, altering or influencing that which has gone before us, we can also travel into the future and interact with our future selves too!

This is one of the best things about energy work: when we operate energetically, time and space become pliable. We are no longer restricted by purely physical constraints, we can transcend the limitations of the linear reality we seem trapped in. In this way, we really do enter the shaman's world – a magical world, the world we would really want to live in, a world of wonder and infinite possibility.

We can do this without psychedelic drugs, without hypnosis and without years of esoteric training – no props or rituals are necessary. We can access these other realms in an 'eyes-open' state of relaxed focus of attention. How magical is that?

When to use the aspect model

It is not always necessary to use the aspect model, and it is not always necessary to talk in such terms to the client. There are times, however, when the aspect model is useful. When a person has experienced an unpleasant situation in their lives, for example a car accident, then it is remarkably helpful and comforting for the client to realise that the event did not actually in reality happen to the person who is now concerned with this issue: it was a past 'aspect' of them. This in itself may come as a surprise and relief. It takes the edge off the intensity. It helps prevent reliving the trauma, which could cause possible unpleasant emotions in the form of abreaction. Moreover, it removes the client from being too identified with the past memories of the accident, leading them towards what psychologists term the 'disassociated state'. (If a client identifies fully with that past memory, psychologists call this an 'associated state'. Seeing the situation through the eyes of the aspect helps keep him in a state of disassociated identification, which is preferable in this case.)

Because the concept of aspects is somewhat esoteric in nature, it is not always a good idea to explain past events in this way. However, it is a concept that often even the most hardened materialist is able to appreciate and accept, more easily than you might imagine when dealing with guilt, regret and severe trauma. In these cases, the aspect model is highly recommended, as it is much easier to love and forgive an aspect of yourself or another than it is to totally love or forgive your now self. To love your aspects and to forgive other people's aspects is a very healing and worthy pursuit for all concerned.

Rescuing and empowering aspects

Another significant part of aspects is the concept that past energy disturbances within the Energy Body affects all future aspects' Energy Bodies and Minds. In order to have free-flowing energy, all aspects need to be free from energy disturbances. With the aspects model we have the tools and understanding required to rescue and empower past and future aspects of others and ourselves.

Let's consider a scenario where an aspect called William has a fear of public speaking. He has had this phobia since he was a child. After a couple of rounds of EFT he feels calm enough to be able to offer us a 'well-formed story' of the precise event that he feels is responsible for his public speaking problem. As a ten-year-old boy he was caught stealing goods from the local shop and as a punishment his teacher made him confess his theft in front of the entire school assembly.

This had caused him to freak out and since then he has never been able to forgive himself or his teacher, or feel comfortable talking in front of people since then. He has asked you to help him because he has just been offered a managerial promotion where he is required to give presentations in front of his Managing Director.

By explaining to William that he is not actually ten years old anymore (William is a six foot five, 40-year-old soon to be sales manager), and that the little boy is an aspect of William who needs to be tapped on to remove all that trapped energy, will serve as a relief to William. We now go into William's past to the precise school assembly event, to comfort that aspect and lovingly tap on his behalf. sufficient EFT rounds to bring about a Healing Event. We may also lovingly tap on the form teacher aspect and even possibly the shopkeeper aspect. When we return to the practitioner's room, all aspects of this story feel completely free from any disturbances and William as a 40-year-old no longer has a fear of public speaking.

Here is an example of using the aspect model within EFT to interact with and change William's future. In his next session, he states that he is looking forward to making a speech on the following Monday – there is no longer any serious energy disturbance there – yet he is keen to make a dynamic impression on his new boss. So it's a wonderful opportunity for both William and the practitioner to go into the future to that Monday morning meeting and support his future aspect by tapping a round or two of EFT to energise and empower him.

Interestingly, William reports back one week later to say that the meeting had been a fantastic experience and his aspect not only excelled in his talk, but that he had also felt an amazing energy flowing through him and in his imagination he actually witnessed two energy beings standing next to him while he was making his address. 'I couldn't help smiling,' he remarked, 'they were standing there tapping on my head! It was more real than I can put into words. This stuff is awesome!'

William could have more accurately recounted his story this way: 'My aspect couldn't help smiling. They (past aspects of me and you) were standing there tapping on my aspect's head! It was more real than I can now put into words.'

Energy Body events

According to Hartmann, all problems begin at an exact time, in a precise place, in a specific single moment. This is an energetic flash – a lightning flash that shoots through the Energy Body – however, it is unable to complete its course and gets stuck somewhere within the energy system. If that energy had been allowed to flow freely through the Energy Body then there would have been no resulting problem. The problem begins to exist at that precise moment when the blockage takes place and continues to be a problem, until that particular energy event is resolved by freeing the trapped, blocked, disturbed energy. If this is a serious blockage with a serious resulting problem, then that exact moment in time and space is called a Genesis Event.

The skilful use of EFT is required to go back to the Genesis Event and to tap that blockage away. When we discover the Genesis Event and take the stuck energy to its ultimate conclusion then we have a Healing Event. This is when the energy blockage is completely removed, allowing the trapped energy to complete its natural course.

Forensic EFT

It's not always easy to discover the Genesis Event, so Hartmann has created a methodology to facilitate this, which she calls Forensic EFT. We conduct Forensic EFT to discover the Genesis Event in the following way. By clever questioning, it is possible to unlock a memory that leads us to the Genesis Event. To the uninitiated this seems to be like magic, even a party trick! With practice, it is surprisingly easy to do.

Here is a simple example of how to do this. (Before we start our story it may be useful to explain to the reader that the presenting problem – the reason why the person has come for EFT help – is not so relevant. It doesn't really matter what the problem is (in this case, a fear of flickering light); what we are focusing on here is how to use precise questioning to arrive at the Genesis Event.)

Angus and his best friend, Alice, arrived for their appointment one afternoon. They apologised for being late due to the inclement foggy weather.

'Sorry we're late,' said an out-of-breath woman, 'We lost our bearings because of the fog.' She introduced a rather introspective man, surprisingly wearing sunglasses. Apparently Angus and Alice had been best friends on the golfing circuit where they had met many years ago.

Once the introductions had been attended to, the session began. It goes without saying that Angus had divulged his phobic response to bright flickering light previously, when making arrangements for his EFT appointment. We join the session as Forensic EFT is about to begin...

'When did all this begin?'

Angus shifted position nervously and his sandy moustache began twitching as he pulled quizzical faces while scratching the back of his head. He mumbled, 'I haven't the faintest idea.'

He then rolled his eyes to the top of his head a couple of times as if to access the repressed memory.

'Was it before you were five years old?'

'No, it was much later than that.'

Angus then added, 'I believe I may have been at boarding school.'

His demeanour noticeably brightened as he sat forward in his chair.

'Now I come to think of it I was indeed at boarding school.'

'Was this in your first year at boarding school?'

Angus emphatically said 'Yes it was'.

He was now becoming quite excited because only a few moments previously he had been adamant that he couldn't remember the details of when he first developed the phobia. And yet, something deep inside him was stirring his long repressed memory of how and when it all began. There was a definite shift of energy recognised by all three of us.

'Was it at the beginning of your first term, or later?'

Angus could not remember, so I asked him whether it had been in the autumn, winter, spring or summer. Then Angus remembered that it had been in the summer.

'You know, I recall it was a scorching hot summer. The grass was dry and the colour of brown shrivelled leaves. We were outside by the golf course and there had been a fire.'

'Who was with you?'

Angus froze and started to cry.

'Now I remember.' he sobbed. 'There were three of us and we had been drinking cider and fooling around. I foolishly lit a cigarette and carelessly tossed the match away. The grass was like tinder and it had exploded into flame. It was at this precise point that I freaked out and literally fainted!'

This clearly was the precise moment when the energy disturbance took place; with careful questioning we had reached the Genesis Event successfully! Now, with the Genesis Event having been found, we begin to use EFT to tap on this memory in order to reach a Healing Event, so as to remove Angus's fear of flickering intense bright light.

Echoes

A Genesis Event that is not dealt with can produce Echoes. This is where the disturbance keeps reappearing. This can actually be helpful to the practitioner because repeated events in the form of Echoes often serve as a doorway to the Genesis Event. If we tap on an Echo then that may be sufficient to deal with the entire problem, as Craig's Generalisation Effect could take place.

A person experiencing repeated Echoes needs to deal with the Genesis Event. The Echoes are symptoms of the original energy disturbance.

Guiding Stars

When dealing with EFT, one could easily be mistaken for believing that all problems stem from some kind of traumatic event. However, this may not always be the case and in some circumstances problems can arise from events that on the surface of things may appear to be pleasurable, enjoyable and positive experiences. These experiences can negatively impact on a person's life. Here are a couple of accessible examples:

- The person who places their first ever £10 bet on the horses at 100 to 1 wins, after which they are hopelessly and helplessly addicted to gambling.

- The person who goes to a party feeling shy and inhibited is offered a chemical substance such as cocaine and instantly is transformed into a prince or a princess.

These examples are fairly common ways that a person can experience addiction and are formed through a Guiding Star.

Hartmann developed the term Guiding Stars, which mirrors the trauma event in that it is an energetic lightning bolt that flashes through the energy system at a specific moment; it gets blocked from completely going through the Energy Body and explodes! What differentiates it from a traumatic event is that the energy flash feels wonderful rather than horrible to the person experiencing it. Here are a few more examples to help understand the idea behind

Guiding Stars where a person's initial experience of wonder and awe can cause them to continually wish to re-experience that magical moment and in so doing they get stuck in a repetitive cycle of behaviour they seem unable to escape from:

- Harry's fetish for custard tarts!
- Matthew's irrepressible and unhealthy longing for blue Italian handbags!
- Peter Pan's refusal to grow up!
- Miss Havisham's wedding day!

Guiding Stars is an advanced energy concept and it offers the EFT practitioner a fascinating insight into how abnormal habits and behaviours such as addictions and fetishes can be formed. It also shows that not all emotional problems are trauma based. EnergyEFT deals with Guiding Stars by finding the Genesis Event (when the Guiding Star is first formed) and tapping away the energy blockage, taking the stuck energy to its natural evolution. Once this is achieved and we hit a Healing Event, the problem that may have dogged a person for a very long time, causing substantial misery to themselves and others, can vanish and the person can be freed from it.

Energetic entities

EnergyEFT deals with energy – 'It is only energy!' is a mantra well understood and frequently spoken by Energists. All relationships are energy relationships. There is no exception to this fact. Everything is energy according to Hartmann, Einstein and shamans alike.

Forming energetic relationships with each other, and with animate and inanimate objects, is perfectly natural for all of us. According to Hartmann, that is how we relate to the world around us. When we communicate with humans, plants, animals, beings from other worlds, computers, cars, corporations, foods, drinks and pop stars, we do not communicate directly, we form an energy entity and relate to that instead. We never have a relationship with someone or something; we have an energy relationship rather than a physical relationship.

The notion of energetic entities may appear esoteric, other worldly and more relevant to a science fiction film/ movie, nevertheless it is observable in everyday encounters. When a person falls in love, they often experience confusion because when they think about this person they feel a certain way, and yet when they meet that person physically they often do not quite seem to be the same. There is a clear mismatch between what we imagine the person to be and what they actually appear to be when we are face to face with them.

We have all experienced people with a fondness for a particular food such chocolate or cheese and they talk about it as if it were their best friend: 'I love chocolate', 'I adore cheese'. We have all met someone who treats their car better than their partner and who gets turned on by their red Ferrari or cute little Mini and swear it's more enjoyable to drive their car than do anything else. Captains are renowned for having a particular relationship to their beloved ships. How many of us have pets? How many of us hate our computers that keep crashing and deleting things when we are not looking? Think about all those teenage infatuations with film/movie stars, etc. There is a myriad of everyday examples like these that sum up the way relationships with energetic entities work.

A note on the relevance of energetic entities

It is useful to see these 'energy personifications' as real and not imaginary or metaphors. We are dealing with energy forms. This is important because we need to be clear about this; these energetic entities do exist. Every religion has a place for non-physical beings such as spirits, ghosts, angels and demons. Very advanced teachers such as Christ accepted this as fact and often healed folk from that perspective. Shamanism does the same.

Practical EFT dealing with energy entities

Sometimes people create energetic entities out of their problems, for example, a lady who says that her obsessive compulsive disorder (OCD) makes her tidy up her room even when it doesn't need to be tidied up and punishes her if she doesn't check 100 times a day to see whether she has left the gas stove on.

If a person presents a problem such as a drug addiction, they may describe their relationship in such terms: 'I feel that there is this monkey on my back.' As an EFT practitioner, we could then use this to form a Set Up to help the client have a better relationship with this entity and ultimately to free it by tapping it away.

A final observation: having an appreciation of energy entities is useful for another significant reason. A person talking in terms of their 'demons' can be frightening to an inexperienced practitioner, especially if they begin to manifest this at the session. Now we have a way of dealing with such problems that is structural and beneficial to both parties. We use EFT to deal with this energy disturbance by tapping it away.

What is emotion, really?

EFT stands for Emotional Freedom Techniques. So, what exactly is emotion? Let's have some fun for a moment – take a good look at this word *emotional*:

Can you see what it contains?

Tune into the frequency of this word.

Now can you see what it contains?

It is: *E (nergy) in motion!*

Hartmann puts it like this: whatever you are experiencing is just energy – 'It's only energy'. If it's flowing freely, we have positive experiences. If it is stuck energy, we may experience negative sensations. Moreover, we experience energy as having different levels of intensity.

The sixth sense

We may observe very subtle energy in a number of ways: kinaesthetically as fine tingles, twitches and shivers; visually as flashes of light and colour around the body; auditory sounds of music and voices; gustatory sensations of taste; and olfactory smells and fragrances. Energists call all this the sixth sense. Energy-sensitive people such as clairvoyants can experience this energy and acquire information from it; we as practitioners of EFT can do the same by learning how to tune into these finer energy vibrations in order to receive valuable feedback when conducting EnergyEFT.

When the energy becomes more obvious and we feel it more strongly, we can be said to be experiencing emotions. In EFT we help stuck energy to move. When energy begins moving, the information held within this energy begins to become ever more accessible, recognisable and apparent to us. This is where we begin to move our client and ourselves from confusion and lack of understanding around a problem to clarity, knowledge and ultimately wisdom.

If the energy becomes stuck or blocked, it is important to realise that it is still attempting to move. Its natural impetus is to be in motion. Long-term blockages of energy can have a serious negative impact on the Energy Body and eventually may lead to physical disturbances – we call these psychosomatic disorders and this is where physical pain may result.

The Mindful EFT Protocol

The Mindful EFT Protocol is about focusing intently on an object that represents the problem. It can be particularly useful for clients with all kinds of relationship challenges. In these cases we could use an artefact such as a letter or a photograph and tap directly on that in order to bring about healing. Other examples could be a glass of water to represent alcohol. Additionally, we could write the name of an addictive substance such as chocolate or ice cream on a piece of paper and tap on that.

When we recognise that we are dealing with energy and the information that it contains, it becomes easier to accept that all manner of things are basically energy. Then, a wide variety of innovative ways of interacting with this energy, such as the examples offered in this chapter, open up before you and that makes working with energy both interesting and fun!

9

Putting the Energy into EFT

The Practical Benefits of Energy Utilisation

We have now come quite a long way on our EFT journey. We have seen where EFT came from and its roots in ancient Chinese energy concepts. We have described how Callahan created the first meridian tapping technique and how Craig popularised the technique by simplifying it and making it accessible to ordinary people on a global basis. We have looked at some of the concepts and techniques of Hartmann – the most advanced and cutting edge EFT practitioner presently at work. It is perhaps now worth taking a moment to reflect on all you have learned and to begin to think about how you can apply EFT to your own life. EFT can be used in an extraordinarily wide variety of situations and issues. This chapter aims to give an outline of some of the more common applications of EFT, which will hopefully be enough to at least get you started in putting your own energy into EnergyEFT work.

In this chapter we will be using the tapping techniques of the three main players discussed in this book: Callahan, Craig and Hartmann. All three of these techniques can be enormously beneficial, and none of them is superior to the others. It would be erroneous to think that any one of these methods has been superseded by the others; they can all be used on any problem or issue that you may wish to tap on and they all have their own advantages. The technique that an individual will favour can be down to personal preference. It may be that you will want to use different techniques for different types of issues that you wish to tap, it's just a matter of finding what happens to work best for you at any particular moment. This is what makes EFT so great to use – it's enormously flexible. There is even a place for random tapping; one of our maxims is: 'Just tap and see!' Whatever challenges you have, by using your intuition in the way that Callahan first discovered tapping – by tapping under Mary's eye – you can experiment with EFT and achieve surprising results. However, if you are trying to deal with a complex or particularly traumatic problem, it is probably best to seek professional guidance. Also remember that if someone comes to you with a physical complaint, it is important that they should first see a doctor about the problem before using EFT.

During this chapter we will therefore invite you to tap on a particular problem using all three methodologies so that you can decide for yourself which approach suits you the best, or maybe you will love all three! Having said this, there are some issues that may be best treated by one particular technique and so we will also provide you with some examples specific to a particular methodology. This is especially appropriate when dealing with the positive side of an issue, when using Hartmann's SUE scale really comes into its own.

Dr Roger Callahan

We are now going to give you an example of one of Callahan's algorithms at work. The following algorithm is for simple anxiety/stress (this is adapted from his book *Tapping the Healer Within: Using Thought Field Therapy to Instantly Conquer*

Your Fears, Anxieties and Emotional Distress (Callahan 2001). Note: this is a slightly abbreviated version of Callahan's. The procedure is as follows:

- We must tune into the problem.

- Measure your place on the SUD scale – from ten to zero.

- Tap on the karate chop point about 15 times.

- Taking two fingers tap five to seven times under the eye.

- Tap under the arm five to seven times.

- Tap on the collarbone position five to seven times.

- Take another reading on the SUD scale to see what improvement has been made.

- Carry out the 9 Gamut Procedure: continue to tap the triple burner (the spot on the back of the hand below and between the little finger and the ring finger). The nine actions are as follows:

  1. Open eyes.

  2. Close eyes.

  3. Eyes point down left.

  4. Eyes point down right.

  5. Roll eyes in one direction.

  6. Roll eyes in opposite direction.

  7. Hum a few notes of any tune.

  8. Count from one to five.

  9. Repeat the humming.

- Tap under the eye again five to seven times

- Tap under the arm again five to seven times

- Tap on the collarbone position again five to seven times

- Take another SUD scale reading. You will now hopefully be down to zero. If not then repeat the above sequence again.

If you are now at zero there is a nice Callahan finish to proceedings, which he calls the floor to ceiling eye roll. This is used when the SUD scale reading is at two to zero. You begin by looking out at a level gaze and allow the eyes to drift down to the floor while keeping the head level and steady. Then tap on the gamut point situated on the back of the hand (the triple burner) while moving the eyes slowly up towards the ceiling.

(One of the authors likes to use this algorithm in conjunction with the collarbone breathing exercise, which he finds particularly effective for general stress relief. Interestingly Callahan discusses the heart rate variable (HRV) at length in his book. The HRV is the space between each heartbeat and he uses a device to measures this. When the space between the heartbeat is at its optimum rate then we are functioning at our best. One of the authors has one such device (a small portable device called a Heartmath and has used it with the collarbone breathing exercise). He has found that this technique does indeed work in the way Callahan claims. It is a very effective way of reducing stress levels and fine-tuning the body when used with the tapping process.)

Gary Craig

We will now apply the Craig EFT protocol to the same stress problem as above. The procedure will be as follows:

- Take a reading on the SUD scale.

- Create the Set Up: 'Even though I have this stress/anxiety, I deeply and completely love and accept myself.' Say this while rubbing the 'sore spot' (collarbone position).

- Carry out the following tapping sequence:

    1.   Eyebrow point (EB).

    2.   Side of the eye (SE).

    3.   Under the eye (UE).

    4.   Under the nose (UN).

    5.   Chin (CH).

    6.   Collarbone (CB).

    7.   Under the arm (UA).

    8.   The hand sequence – starting with the outside edge of the thumb, systematically tap each finger, while omitting the ring finger.

    9.   Finish with the karate chop point (KC).

- After the first round of tapping, take another measurement on the SUD. If the problem has completely disappeared and you are down to zero – congratulations! Otherwise repeat an amended Set Up sentence such as: 'Even though I still have some of this stress/anxiety, I deeply and completely love and accept myself', while rubbing the 'sore spot' (collarbone position).

- Repeat another tapping round following the tapping sequence outlined above.

- Repeat further rounds until the problem has been completely removed.

If further rounds do not remove the problem, try out the 9 Gamut Procedure as in Callahan's TFT protocol and the original Craig recipe.

Dr Silvia Hartmann

We now use Hartmann's EnergyEFT procedure on the same stress problem.

- First, you are invited to stand up for all Hartmann EFT sessions.

- Measure your position on Hartmann's SUE scale (minus ten to plus ten).

- Move into the heart healing position by placing your hands on the centre of the chest, take a deep breath and say 'Stress' or 'De-stress' as the set-up sentence.

- In the Heart and Soul Protocol there are 14 tapping points. They begin on the top of the head and conveniently follow the body downwards as follows:

  1. Top of the head.

  2. Forehead (third eye point).

  3. Eyebrow.

  4. Side of eye.

  5. Under the eye.

  6. Above the lip.

  7. Under the lip/the chin position.

  8. Collarbone.

  9. A walk around the hand starting with the thumb.

10. First/index finger.

11. Second finger.

12. Ring finger.

13. Little finger.

14. End with the karate chop position.

- The reminder phrase to use while tapping in this case will be the same: 'Stress'. (Readers who have paid attention so far will notice the omission of the under the arm position, the addition of the third eye point and the use of the ring finger.)

- Return to the heart position and takes three deep breaths. Now take another measurement on the SUE scale.

- Carry out further rounds of EFT until you reach zero on the SUE scale.

- Proceed with the aim of moving up to the positive side of the SUE scale. It is now appropriate to stop tapping on stress and tap on something positive, for example energy, success, etc.

- Carry out the same tapping sequence as above but with the new Set Up sentence.

- Continue with rounds of tapping until you have reached a high position on the SUE scale.

Having now tried all three techniques on the same problem, have a go at answering the following questions:

1. Which one of the three did you find the most useful and why?

2. Was there an obvious one that stood out for you (a favourite) or did you like all of them equally?

3. Which one did you find easiest to use?

4. Which one did you find most difficult to use?

5. Did you get similar results between all three or did they vary significantly?

6. What did you learn?

7. What would you do differently next time?

8. Would you use EFT in the future to reduce stress?

Record your findings in your EFT notebook

Applications of EFT

Here is a list of common problems that you can use EnergyEFT to solve:

- accelerated learning
- addictions
- affirmations
- agoraphobia
- alcohol challenges
- anger management
- anxiety
- bed wetting
- belief formation
- bereavement
- bliss
- compulsions
- confidence
- cravings
- creativity
- curses and spells
- depression
- dreams and aspirations
- energy
- enlightenment
- exhaustion

- expanding consciousness
- fatigue
- fear
- forgiveness
- ghosts and apparitions
- goal orientation
- god
- gratitude
- grief
- hair pulling
- headaches
- Irritable Bowel Syndrome (IBS)
- insomnia
- jealousy
- joy
- learning disorders
- love
- low self-esteem
- lucid dreaming
- memory
- menstruation
- mental illness
- migraines
- money problems
- motivation
- nail biting
- nightmares
- Obsessive Compulsive Disorder (OCD)
- opposite sex
- pain
- performing arts
- pets
- phobias
- Post-Traumatic Stress Disorder (PTSD)
- premature ejaculation
- public speaking
- relationships
- self-harming
- sexual abuse
- shamanism
- shyness
- skin disorders
- smoking
- spirits
- spirituality

- sports performance
- stammering and speech impediments
- stress
- Tourette's syndrome
- transcendence
- trauma
- wealth creation
- weight issues
- writer's block.

This is by no means an exhaustive list, but is an indication of the range of subjects that EFT can be applied to.

Exploring the positive side of the SUE scale

Emotional Freedom Techniques (and its precursor Thought Field Therapy) was originally developed to solve emotional problems and is still extensively used to remove emotional issues; this is what it is known for and what it is good for. EFT excels in treating such emotional challenges.

In terms of Western mindsets, we still only consider visiting the doctor when we have something wrong with us. We rarely, if ever, visit a doctor when we are experiencing optimum health to discuss or seek expert advice on how to feel even better!

EFT has evolved since its inception and currently it is at a place in its development where it is extending its frontiers beyond remedial therapy and moving more towards optimising a person's physical, emotional and spiritual wellbeing. This is cutting-edge philosophy, and we are living in an exciting era where the old model of the human condition of mediocrity (feeling 'okayness') is being challenged.

Practical applications of non-remedial EFT

By turning our attention to the previous list we can see that a number of topics would readily fit into this category:

- accelerated learning
- bliss
- dreams and aspirations
- enlightenment
- energy
- expanding consciousness
- god
- joy
- love
- lucid dreaming
- motivation
- performing arts
- relationships
- sports performance
- transcendence
- wealth creation.

For the purposes of our demonstration, we shall use *energy* along with Hartmann's Heart and Soul Protocol.

The Heart and Soul Protocol in action

To start our round of EnergyEFT, we begin in the heart healing position by placing our hands on the centre of the chest. This is the position we always start from and finish with. The tapping points begin on the top of the head, next is the forehead (third eye point), eyebrow, side of eye, under the eye, above the lip (affectionately called the shaving foam position), under the lip/the chin position, collarbone and then a walk around the hand starting with the thumb, first/index finger, second finger, ring finger ('God gave us five fingers'), little finger, and ends with karate chop position.

To begin the session, before proceeding to tap we need to activate our 'healing hands' by shaking them, clapping them, blowing on them and briskly rubbing them together. This helps create our intention and focuses our attention on the task. This should be done in a loving playful manner with pleasant smiles on our faces to evoke a spirit of warmth and gentleness.

Next we turn our attention to the Set Up by placing our hands in the healing heart position. We now take three deep breaths and make the first Set Up statement out loud.

The Set Up statement is a sentence in the present tense that describes the issue in its most general, immediate terms. In our example: 'Energy'. Now we begin to tap. We can use either hand and, as the body is symmetrical, we can tap on either side of the head and body.

We begin to tap on the phrase: 'Energy'. As the round develops and our energetic frequency increases, travelling further and higher along the SUE scale, we may change this phrase to other more specific energy words such as: 'Golden energy', 'Healing energy', 'Loving energy', 'Miraculous energy', 'Powerful energy', etc. We do this to express our feelings, thoughts and intuitions that flow freely from this energy interaction. This is a form of EFT free flow and you can change the phrases to match the experience, thus potentiating the EFT round, pushing it further and further up towards the positive higher end of the scale.

At the completion of the round the person returns to the heart healing position and takes three deep breaths. An assessment is now made to see what has changed. EFT can have such a powerful, immediate effect on a person, that a single round or even less can completely energise the participant. The aim is to keep tapping until you reach plus ten on the SUE scale.

Now pick a subject from the above list and have a go on your own (or with a friend). You may use the Heart and Soul Protocol. See if you can reach the higher end of the SUE scale.

1. What did you learn from this exercise?

2. How useful was this exercise?

3. How could you improve your EFT experience?

4. How will you use this technique in the future?

Write your answers in your EFT notebook.

Taking EFT into our future

Craig has always believed that EFT could take us into enlightened places spiritually speaking – it could be argued that this is the sublime goal of EFT – to take humanity onwards and upwards to a new stage of spiritual evolution. If this sounds a little grandiose, let's reconsider our personal example of Chapter 6 where one of the authors (Paul Millward) experiences EFT for the first time: 'As the tapping continued, I fell into ecstasy – I was dancing with angels, floating in a heavenly realm of light and bliss.' This account seems to suggest that these new ambitious claims and the orientation of EFT are possible and certainly rooted in subjective experience.

Hartmann's SUE scale stands for and measures Subjective Units of Experience. The positive side of this scale offers an instrument to both facilitate and monitor higher states of being (plus eight, plus nine, plus ten). Whereas Craig talks about optimum functioning and spiritual enlightenment, Hartmann provides us with a practical tool in the SUE scale to quantify such high energy states within the context of an EFT session.

The result of this allows a way for EFT to systematically shift from focusing on the negative aspects of the human experience (away from remedial consideration), taking it into the higher energetic frequencies of the positive spiritual states of wellbeing and beyond.

10

A Client's Perspective of a Professional EFT/ EnergyEFT Session

During the course of this book we have looked at how you can theoretically and practically carry out EFT on your own or with a partner. This may be sufficient for all the problems or issues that you wish to deal with and you may not ever want or need to receive guidance from a professional EFT practitioner. However, you may know people who you think would benefit from some professional EFT, or you may yourself have a particular problem that you do not feel confident enough to handle on your own without professional assistance.

Moreover, as early as Chapter 4 and specifically in Chapter 6 and beyond, we have introduced the notion that EFT is evolving and progressing towards the idea that EFT can be used to improve any aspect of one's life and take it to a level of excellence, rather than solely concentrating on removing remedial issues. In fact, in theory, there are no restrictions to what EFT can be applied to in order to transform our lives and achieve our wildest dreams. This is why it could benefit everyone to seek the assistance of a qualified practitioner. This chapter is designed to help you to choose a suitable professional and to give you an idea of what to expect from a professional EFT session.

What to look for in a professional tapping capacity

First, it may be helpful to remind the reader that there are at least three main forms that influence tapping: Callahan's TFT, Craig's EFT and Hartmann's EnergyEFT. All are excellent and do a good job. They all are based around tapping to remove energy disturbances. On a practical level, it makes sense to visit a local practitioner and therefore the person you choose to help you may use any of these methods and even a mixture of them. That is perfectly fine.

With today's technology, it is fairly easy to find a practitioner. The internet is a good place to start. Check for website presence and get a feel for what is on offer.

Then why not phone the practitioner to book an initial consultation? Often these are free. This will give you the opportunity to discuss your issue, their fees, etc. It is advisable to trust your intuition. Was the person approachable, friendly and someone you could feel comfortable with? If so, fantastic – you are ready, go for it! If not, then politely decline and search for another professional.

Obviously, one of the best ways to choose a therapist is by personal recommendation of family members or friends, or a referral from your local GP. Do bear in mind that folk do not always want to disclose the fact that they have seen a therapist, and confidentiality is a must for the professional EFTer. However, there are times when people are happy to talk about their EFT experiences and recommend the practitioner; this is certainly helpful and benefits all concerned.

At the time of writing this book, EFT in the UK is unregulated; this means that there is no government legislation controlling the practice of EFT. Therefore, anyone is at liberty to call him or herself an EFT professional and set up in business in the UK. This, however, is not necessarily the case in the rest of the world and readers are advised to check this out in their own country or region of residence.

Professional qualifications may be a useful guide to professional competence. It would be unusual for a serious practitioner not to have pursued some form of official training; however, it is not advisable to base your decision purely on qualifications, as it is possible to have stacks of certificates and to wear a suit and tie and not necessarily be good at practically helping someone. (How does wearing a suit make you a good accountant? Paul would love to know the answer to that!)

Additionally, palatial offices in grandiose buildings do not have to be a decisive factor. Practitioners may practise in the comfort and modesty of their homes, and while a fancy office may guarantee expensive treatment sessions, it is not necessarily an indication of expertise or superiority. What we are looking for is a genuine, caring person who is primarily practising EFT out of their love to help you, not in the business of just making business! Rather than judging a book by its cover, feel your way to the right person! We are energetic beings having energetic relationships and since the 1960s the world has been moving away from traditional rigid formality to a more relaxed democratic society; this should be reflected in the business world. As long as the practitioner comes over as being knowledgeable in their chosen field of practice, intelligent and caring then this should be sufficient to indicate that they have the kinds of attributes you are looking for.

Following on from this thought, one indication of a practitioner's merit could be the length of time they have been practising. An EFT practitioner would probably not survive very long if they were not good at what they did. However, do not discount a newcomer to EFT – we all have to start somewhere. Someone will always be our first ever client! A fresh, enthusiastic EFT practitioner is always a positive sign you are on the right track.

How to handle your initial free phone inquiry

All the above advice now comes into play. Be friendly and personable; by all means ask questions; however, centre the conversation on you and your issue, rather than treating it as looking to employ someone. The following questions are not the best ones to open with: How long have you been practising? What qualifications do you have? What's your success rate? Asking a professional these questions may be considered somewhat condescending. Would you ask these types of questions to a doctor, a dentist or a solicitor? One of the authors once foolishly asked a Roman Catholic minister how long he had been a Father. 'Oh ages!' he sarcastically replied!

Asking appropriate questions that focus on you and your issue is the right way to go: Can you help me with my problem? What time can we meet up? How much will each session cost? How long does each session take? Obviously, later in your relationship when you have got to know the therapist a little better, you could casually ask more challenging questions such as those mentioned above.

General reasons for seeing a professional

These will be emotional disturbances and problems that you cannot personally handle. Sometimes it's just better, more convenient and more helpful to have another perspective on a problem. Maybe you have tried to deal with the issue (with or without EFT). Additionally you may have already been to see a doctor without too much success, or if you have a more open-minded doctor, they may have recommended that you see an EFT specialist.

Here is another look at our Chapter 8 list of problems that could be dealt with by an EFT practitioner:

- accelerated learning
- addictions
- affirmations
- agoraphobia
- alcohol challenges
- anger management
- anxiety
- bed wetting
- belief formation
- bereavement
- bliss
- compulsions
- confidence
- cravings
- creativity
- curses and spells
- depression
- dreams and aspirations
- energy
- enlightenment
- exhaustion
- expanding consciousness
- fatigue
- fear
- forgiveness
- ghosts and apparitions
- goal orientation
- god
- gratitude
- grief
- hair pulling
- headaches
- Irritable Bowel Syndrome (IBS)
- insomnia
- jealousy
- joy
- learning disorders
- love
- low self-esteem
- lucid dreaming
- memory

- menstruation
- mental illness
- migraines
- money problems
- motivation
- nail biting
- nightmares
- Obsesssive Compulsive Disorder (OCS)
- opposite sex
- pain
- performing arts
- pets
- phobias
- Post-Traumatic Stress Disorder (PTSD)
- premature ejaculation
- public speaking
- relationships
- self-harming
- sexual abuse
- shamanism
- shyness
- skin disorders
- smoking
- spirits
- spirituality
- sports performance
- stammering and speech impediments
- stress
- Tourette's syndrome
- transcendence
- trauma
- wealth creation
- weight issues
- writer's block.

This is by no means an exhaustive list, but is an indication of the range of subjects that EFT can be applied to.

Conditions conducive to a successful EFT session

The ideal EFT session would take place in a relaxed and friendly atmosphere. The session would be a minimum of 45 minutes; one to two hours would be better. This would be sufficient time to develop a rewarding relationship in which you could feel safe and happy that your problem was being professionally treated. It is important to bear in mind that the problem may not be solved in a single session and to be prepared to have a number of sessions if necessary.

In normal circumstances, it is preferable to attend the sessions on your own. In the majority of cases, this works best for both client and therapist. However, if you are particularly nervous, it might be advisable to take someone along with you to the session and the therapist will normally be okay with this.

If the client is a child then in the UK it is necessary for an adult to accompany them. (Check your own country for specific guidelines.)

The issue of confidentiality is an important one. The client needs to be confident that what they share in any session remains in the session.

It is fairly standard practice for the practitioner to explain the EFT process before commencing actual tapping. Again it's important to stress that this is a democratic adult relationship, so if you require further explanation of anything do ask!

The EFT session needs to take you towards a Healing Event. As long as the treatment is positively flowing in that direction then the session can be considered to be a success. It is extremely rare for EFT to make your problem worse rather than better; the worst-case scenario would be little obvious change or benefit of the EFT time spent together. Be prepared to persevere. Do not assume that if little headway has occurred in a particular session, that nothing positive has happened. Sometimes a number of sessions are necessary. As a very basic guideline, if no positive results have occurred after, say, three sessions then it might be worth reappraising the situation.

Do financially commit to your EFT sessions. Consider them an investment of time and money. Whereas there are therapists who offer free services, and all of us have generously given free sessions from time to time, as a general rule do not expect this – you are going to visit a professional and therefore should expect to pay for treatment accordingly. Additionally, a practitioner who is charging reasonable rates is a confident therapist!

As with all mature relationships, one needs to feel confident around interaction; it is okay to have honest exchanges of opinions with inherent agreements and disagreements. EFT is less hierarchical than other forms of therapy. An attitude of 'let's see what we can do to solve this problem together' is favourable.

One of the great things about the development of EFT is the notion that one can foster an on-going relationship with your EFT professional. Rather than seeing him or her as a 'one off' encounter, why not make the most of their services and when a new challenge comes along see it as an opportunity to explore this issue with them? In this sense they become an established helper for you, your family and friends – and that is a wonderful thing!

You may reach a point where you see your EFT sessions as going beyond merely dealing with problems and developing your energy to bring about improvements to your energy system, maximising your state of wellbeing over time. It is certainly beneficial to have periodic top-ups of energy work.

Be prepared to be touched! There may be times where the therapist deems it appropriate to tap directly on the client and they will ask your permission to do so – don't be off-put or surprised by this. It can be deeply healing and reassuring to have a person tap on your behalf! Likewise, in extremely stressful circumstances it may be counterproductive to tap on a person straight away. In this case, other forms of intervention may take place before EFT tapping begins. This could be in the form of breathing exercises, massage, being given a crystal or a cuddly toy, being offered a glass of water, etc. This is perfectly fine; trust that your therapist has your best interests in mind and at heart.

At this point it is beneficial to consider that EFT is a dynamic energetic relationship that can operate on many levels. It is not simply a case of being spoon-fed advice and information. Done well, EFT is often a surprising and novel experience and never contrived. It is about raising your energy sufficiently to enable a distilled clarity of vision to spontaneously emerge as you experience higher and higher levels of coherence and mental, emotional and spiritual integration.

On a more down-to-earth level, expect the practitioner to be human! They go shopping, and have families and hobbies outside of their work. While it is tempting to confer upon them a guru-like status, appreciate that they are fallible human beings like the rest of us!

Ethical considerations towards the therapist
If you make an appointment and for whatever reason change your mind, it is a polite and responsible thing to do to let your therapist know well in advance – either by phoning or texting them – of your decision.

Reasons for going to a professional practitioner other than treating remedial issues

- for advanced EFT – don't go where you're not confident
- when you don't have time to work on issues yourself

- a need for guided motivation
- when more discipline is required to begin or complete a project
- if you wish to become a professional therapist yourself – learning from a master is a great idea
- life coaching
- sports performance
- developing all kinds of performance skills, for example, learning to sing professionally
- to make you aware of things that you can't see yourself
- to examine yourself to make improvements
- synergy – two heads are energetically better than one.

The future of EFT

This book has been principally concerned with charting the historical and practical development of meridian-based tapping techniques such as TFT, EFT and our much-loved EnergyEFT. Way back in the day when EFT was a mere infant, the enthusiastic father, Craig, instantly recognised the prodigious potential of this new-born energy child. In fact he said: 'this is the first floor of a high rise', signifying that EFT has a fabulous future and no one at that time was quite able to predict just what its full potential would be. They were exciting times then and arguably our times now are even more momentous. Energy psychology is still very much in its infancy, yet it has already made some impressive leaps forward fitting aptly within the framework of the perceived paradigm shift that took place at the end of 2012 and continues to lead us further into the new millennium.

One young songwriter of the 1960s, Robert Zimmerman, better known as Bob Dylan, sang 'the times they are a-changin', and that sentiment holds as true today as it did in that past halcyon decade of optimism. We are now living in extraordinary times and EFT is an extraordinary technique that continues not only to live up to its past glory, but also to take us into new uncharted territory where the unfolding potential of humankind can be realised. It is our hope that by reading this book you may also be swept along by the EnergyEFT tide, and we invite you to continue to surf the energy wave along with us into that glorious future.

BIBLIOGRAPHY

Callahan, R.J. (2001) *Tapping the Healer Within: Using Thought Field Therapy to Conquer Your Fears, Anxieties and Emotional Distress.* New York: McGraw Hill.

Castaneda, C. (1981) *The Eagle's Gift.* New York: Simon and Schuster.

Castaneda, C. (1990) *The Teachings of Don Juan: A Yaqui Way of Knowledge.* London: Penguin.

Craig, G. (2011) *EFT (Emotional Freedom Techniques) Manual.* 2nd edn. Santa Rosa, CA: Energy Psychology Press.

Dr Z (Peña, Anthony L.) (2013) *Dr. Carl G. Jung and the Age of Aquarius. The Zodiac Master with Dr Z.* Available online at www.thezodiac. com, accessed on 12 June 2013.

Essick, R.N. and Viscomi, J. (eds) (1988) *The Illuminated Books of William Blake, Volume 5: Milton, A Poem.* Princeton, NJ: Princeton University Press.

Foundation for Inner Peace (1979) *A Course in Miracles.* New York: Viking. (Original work published 1975; Tiburon, CA: Foundations for Inner Peace).

Hartmann, S. (2009) *Events Psychology.* Eastbourne, UK: DragonRising.

Hartmann, S. (2011a). AMT EFT Master Practitioner Course. [Course notes]. Available online at: http://theamt.com/courses/eft_master_practitioner.htm, accessed 16 June 2014.

Hartmann, S. (2011b). *The EFT Master Practitioner's Training Manual.* Eastbourne, UK: DragonRising.

Hartmann, S. (2011c). *Energy EFT (Book & Video): Next Generation Tapping & Emotional Freedom Techniques.* Eastbourne, UK: DragonRising.

Holy Bible New International Version (1983). London: Hodder and Stoughton.

Hartmann, S. (2012) *Energy EFT – Energize Your Life From Minus 10 to Plus 10 With the Essential Next Generation A–Z Field Guide to Self Help EFT.* Eastbourne, UK: DragonRising.

Kerouac, J. (2011) *On the Road.* London: Penguin Essentials. (Original work published 1957; New York, NY: Viking Press).

Lipton, B. (2005) *The Biology of Belief: Unleashing the Power of Consciousness, Matter and Miracles.* Santa Rosa, CA: Elite Books.

Mcluhan, R. (2010) *Randi's Prize: What Sceptics Say About the Paranormal, Why they are Wrong and Why it Matters.* Leicester, UK: Matador.

Pirsig, R.M. (1974) *Zen and the Art of Motorcycle Maintenance.* London: Vintage.

Sheldrake, R. (2012) *The Science Delusion: Freeing the Spirit of Enquiry.* London: Coronet.

Sheldrake, R. [revolutionloveevolve]. (2013, March 15). *Rupert Sheldrake – The Science Delusion, Banned Ted Talk* [Video file]. Available online at www.youtube.com/watch?v=JKHUaNAxsTg.

Wu, Z. (2010) *Chinese Shamanic Cosmic Orbit Qigong: Esoteric Talismans, Mantras and Mudras in Healing and Inner Cultivation.* London: Singing Dragon.

LIST OF ORGANISATIONS
AND USEFUL CONTACTS

- Dr Silvia Hartmann at the AMT: The Association for Meridian and Energy Therapies: www.theamt.com

- Gary Craig's official website: The Gold Standard for EFT: www.emofree.com

- Dr Roger Callahan's official website: www.roger callahan.com

- Lawrence Pagett: www.hypnotherapykidderminster. co.uk

CPI Antony Rowe
Eastbourne, UK
June 29, 2023